THE ENCYCLOPEDIA OF PSYCHOACTIVE DRUGS

SERIES 1

The Addictive Personality
Alcohol and Alcoholism
Alcohol Customs and Rituals
Alcohol Teenage Drinking
Amphetamines Danger in the Fast Lane
Barbiturates Sleeping Potion or Intoxicant?
Caffeine The Most Popular Stimulant
Cocaine A New Epidemic
Escape from Anxiety and Stress
Flowering Plants Magic in Bloom
Getting Help Treatments for Drug Abuse
Heroin The Street Narcotic
Inhalants The Toxic Fumes

LSD Visions or Nightmares?
Marijuana Its Effects on Mind & Body
Methadone Treatment for Addiction
Mushrooms Psychedelic Fungi
Nicotine An Old-Fashioned Addiction
Over-The-Counter Drugs Harmless or Hazardous?
PCP The Dangerous Angel
Prescription Narcotics The Addictive Painkillers
Quaaludes The Quest for Oblivion
Teenage Depression and Drugs
Treating Mental Illness
Valium and Other Tranquilizers

SERIES 2

Bad Trips
Brain Function
Case Histories
Celebrity Drug Use
Designer Drugs
The Downside of Drugs
Drinking, Driving, and Drugs
Drugs and Civilization
Drugs and Crime
Drugs and Diet
Drugs and Disease
Drugs and Emotion
Drugs and Pain
Drugs and Perception
Drugs and Pregnancy
Drugs and Sexual Behavior

Drugs and Sleep
Drugs and Sports
Drugs and the Arts
Drugs and the Brain
Drugs and the Family
Drugs and the Law
Drugs and Women
Drugs of the Future
Drugs Through the Ages
Drug Use Around the World
Legalization: A Debate
Mental Disturbances
Nutrition and the Brain
The Origins and Sources of Drugs
Substance Abuse: Prevention and Treatment
Who Uses Drugs?

DRUGS
&
CIVILIZATION

GENERAL EDITOR
Professor Solomon H. Snyder, M.D.
*Distinguished Service Professor of
Neuroscience, Pharmacology, and Psychiatry at
The Johns Hopkins University School of Medicine*

•

ASSOCIATE EDITOR
Professor Barry L. Jacobs, Ph.D.
*Program in Neuroscience, Department of Psychology,
Princeton University*

•

SENIOR EDITORIAL CONSULTANT
Joann Rodgers
*Deputy Director, Office of Public Affairs at
The Johns Hopkins Medical Institutions*

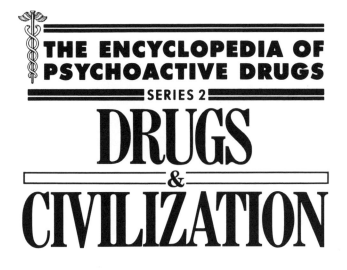

THE ENCYCLOPEDIA OF PSYCHOACTIVE DRUGS
SERIES 2
DRUGS & CIVILIZATION

SALLY FREEMAN

CHELSEA HOUSE PUBLISHERS

NEW YORK • NEW HAVEN • PHILADELPHIA

EDITOR-IN-CHIEF: Nancy Toff
EXECUTIVE EDITOR: Remmel T. Nunn
MANAGING EDITOR: Karyn Gullen Browne
COPY CHIEF: Juliann Barbato
PICTURE EDITOR: Adrian G. Allen
ART DIRECTOR: Giannella Garrett
MANUFACTURING MANAGER: Gerald Levine

Staff for DRUGS AND CIVILIZATION:

SENIOR EDITOR: Jane Larkin Crain
ASSOCIATE EDITOR: Paula Edelson
ASSISTANT EDITOR: Laura-Ann Dolce
COPY EDITOR: Michael Goodman
EDITORIAL ASSISTANT: Susan DeRosa
ASSOCIATE PICTURE EDITOR: Juliette Dickstein
PICTURE RESEARCHER: Ann Levy
DESIGNER: Victoria Tomaselli
DESIGN ASSISTANT: Laura Lang
PRODUCTION COORDINATOR: Joseph Romano

CREATIVE DIRECTOR: Harold Steinberg

First Printing

1 3 5 7 9 8 6 4 2

Library of Congress Cataloging in Publication Data

Freeman, Sally.
  Drugs and Civilization.
    p. cm.—(The Encyclopedia of psychoactive drugs. Series 2)
  Bibliography: p.
  Includes index.
    1. Psychotropic drugs—History—Juvenile literature. 2. Drug utilization—
History—Juvenile literature. 3. Drugs. I. Title. II. Series.
RM315.F74 1988   362.2'932'09—dc19   87-23273   CIP   AC

ISBN 1-55546-222-7

CONTENTS

Drug use has been an integral part of social customs and rituals for millennia. These patrons of a New York bar converse while drinking alcohol, the most widely used — and abused — drug in the world.

FOREWORD

In the Mainstream
of American Life

One of the legacies of the social upheaval of the 1960s is that psychoactive drugs have become part of the mainstream of American life. Schools, homes, and communities cannot be "drug proofed." There is a demand for drugs — and the supply is plentiful. Social norms have changed and drugs are not only available—they are everywhere.

But where efforts to curtail the supply of drugs and outlaw their use have had tragically limited effects on demand, it may be that education has begun to stem the rising tide of drug abuse among young people and adults alike.

Over the past 25 years, as drugs have become an increasingly routine facet of contemporary life, a great many teenagers have adopted the notion that drug taking was somehow a right or a privilege or a necessity. They have done so, however, without understanding the consequences of drug use during the crucial years of adolescence.

The teenage years are few in the total life cycle, but critical in the maturation process. During these years adolescents face the difficult tasks of discovering their identity, clarifying their sexual roles, asserting their independence, learning to cope with authority, and searching for goals that will give their lives meaning.

Drugs rob adolescents of precious time, stamina, and health. They interrupt critical learning processes, sometimes forever. Teenagers who use drugs are likely to withdraw increasingly into themselves, to "cop out" at just the time when they most need to reach out and experience the world.

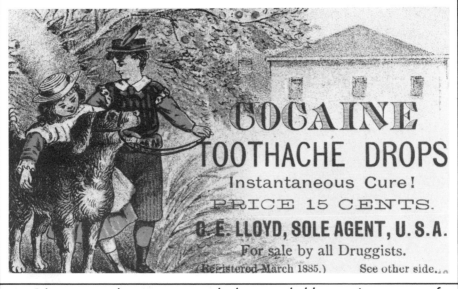

A 19th-century advertisement extols the remarkable curative powers of cocaine. Abuse of cocaine, a drug that was initially hailed as a medical panacea, reached epidemic proportions in the 1980s.

Fortunately, as a recent Gallup poll shows, young people are beginning to realize this, too. They themselves label drugs their most important problem. In the last few years, moreover, the climate of tolerance and ignorance surrounding drugs has been changing.

Adolescents as well as adults are becoming aware of mounting evidence that every race, ethnic group, and class is vulnerable to drug dependency.

Recent publicity about the cost and failure of drug rehabilitation efforts; dangerous drug use among pilots, air traffic controllers, star athletes, and Hollywood celebrities; and drug-related accidents, suicides, and violent crime have focused the public's attention on the need to wage an all-out war on drug abuse before it seriously undermines the fabric of society itself.

The anti-drug message is getting stronger and there is evidence that the message is beginning to get through to adults and teenagers alike.

The Encyclopedia of Psychoactive Drugs hopes to play a part in the national campaign now underway to educate young people about drugs. Series 1 provides clear and comprehensive discussions of common psychoactive substances, outlines their psychological and physiological effects on the mind and body, explains how they "hook" the user, and separates fact from myth in the complex issue of drug abuse.

Whereas Series 1 focuses on specific drugs, such as nicotine or cocaine, Series 2 confronts a broad range of both social and physiological phenomena. Each volume addresses the ramifications of drug use and abuse on some aspect of human experience: social, familial, cultural, historical, and physical. Separate volumes explore questions about the effects of drugs on brain chemistry and unborn children; the use and abuse of painkillers; the relationship between drugs and sexual behavior, sports, and the arts; drugs and disease; the role of drugs in history; and the sophisticated drugs now being developed in the laboratory that will profoundly change the future.

Each book in the series is fully illustrated and is tailored to the needs and interests of young readers. The more adolescents know about drugs and their role in society, the less likely they are to misuse them.

Joann Rodgers
Senior Editorial Consultant

A 1904 photograph of an Alaskan medicine man. Folk remedies involving the use of psychoactive plants have been employed through the ages, often with results as successful as any known to modern medicine.

INTRODUCTION

The Gift of Wizardry
Use and Abuse

JACK H. MENDELSON, M.D.
NANCY K. MELLO, Ph.D.
Alcohol and Drug Abuse Research Center
Harvard Medical School—McLean Hospital

Dorothy to the Wizard:

"I think you are a very bad man," said Dorothy.
"Oh no, my dear; I'm really a very good man; but I'm a very bad Wizard."
—from THE WIZARD OF OZ

Man is endowed with the gift of wizardry, a talent for discovery and invention. The discovery and invention of substances that change the way we feel and behave are among man's special accomplishments, and, like so many other products of our wizardry, these substances have the capacity to harm as well as to help. Psychoactive drugs can cause profound changes in the chemistry of the brain and other vital organs, and although their legitimate use can relieve pain and cure disease, their abuse leads in a tragic number of cases to destruction.

Consider alcohol — available to all and yet regarded with intense ambivalence from biblical times to the present day. The use of alcoholic beverages dates back to our earliest ancestors. Alcohol use and misuse became associated with the worship of gods and demons. One of the most powerful Greek gods was Dionysus, lord of fruitfulness and god of wine. The Romans adopted Dionysus but changed his name to Bacchus. Festivals and holidays associated with Bacchus celebrated the harvest and the origins of life. Time has blurred the images of the Bacchanalian festival, but the theme of drunkenness as a major part of celebration has survived the pagan gods and remains a familiar part of modern society. The term "Bacchanalian Festival" conveys a more appealing image than "drunken orgy" or "pot party," but whatever the label, drinking alcohol is a form of drug use that results in addiction for millions.

The fact that many millions of other people can use alcohol in moderation does not mitigate the toll this drug takes on society as a whole. According to reliable estimates, one out of every ten Americans develops a serious alcohol-related problem sometime in his or her lifetime. In addition, automobile accidents caused by drunken drivers claim the lives of tens of thousands every year. Many of the victims are gifted young people, just starting out in adult life. Hospital emergency rooms abound with patients seeking help for alcohol-related injuries.

Who is to blame? Can we blame the many manufacturers who produce such an amazing variety of alcoholic beverages? Should we blame the educators who fail to explain the perils of intoxication, or so exaggerate the dangers of drinking that no one could possibly believe them? Are friends to blame — those peers who urge others to "drink more and faster," or the macho types who stress the importance of being able to "hold your liquor"? Casting blame, however, is hardly constructive, and pointing the finger is a fruitless way to deal with the problem. Alcoholism and drug abuse have few culprits but many victims. Accountability begins with each of us, every time we choose to use or misuse an intoxicating substance.

It is ironic that some of man's earliest medicines, derived from natural plant products, are used today to poison and to intoxicate. Relief from pain and suffering is one of society's many continuing goals. Over 3,000 years ago, the Therapeutic Papyrus of Thebes, one of our earliest written records, gave instructions for the use of opium in the treatment of pain. Opium, in the form of its major derivative, morphine, and similar compounds, such as heroin, have also been used by many to induce changes in mood and feeling. Another example of man's misuse of a natural substance is the coca leaf, which for centuries was used by the Indians of Peru to reduce fatigue and hunger. Its modern derivative, cocaine, has important medical use as a local anesthetic. Unfortunately, its increasing abuse in the 1980s clearly has reached epidemic proportions.

The purpose of this series is to explore in depth the psychological and behavioral effects that psychoactive drugs have on the individual, and also, to investigate the ways in which drug use influences the legal, economic, cultural, and even moral aspects of societies. The information presented here (and in other books in this series) is based on many clinical and laboratory studies and other observations by people from diverse walks of life.

Over the centuries, novelists, poets, and dramatists have provided us with many insights into the sometimes seductive but ultimately problematic aspects of alcohol and drug use. Physicians, lawyers, biologists, psychologists, and social scientists have contributed to a better understanding of the causes and consequences of using these substances. The authors in this series have attempted to gather and condense all the latest information about drug use and abuse. They have also described the sometimes wide gaps in our knowledge and have suggested some new ways to answer many difficult questions.

One such question, for example, is how do alcohol and drug problems get started? And what is the best way to treat them when they do? Not too many years ago, alcoholics and drug abusers were regarded as evil, immoral, or both. It is now recognized that these persons suffer from very complicated diseases involving deep psychological and social problems. To understand how the disease begins and progresses, it is necessary to understand the nature of the substance, the behavior of addicts, and the characteristics of the society or culture in which they live.

Although many of the social environments we live in are very similar, some of the most subtle differences can strongly influence our thinking and behavior. Where we live, go to school and work, whom we discuss things with — all influence our opinions about drug use and misuse. Yet we also share certain commonly accepted beliefs that outweigh any differences in our attitudes. The authors in this series have tried to identify and discuss the central, most crucial issues concerning drug use and misuse.

Despite the increasing sophistication of the chemical substances we create in the laboratory, we have a long way to go in our efforts to make these powerful drugs work for us rather than against us.

The volumes in this series address a wide range of timely questions. What influence has drug use had on the arts? Why do so many of today's celebrities and star athletes use drugs, and what is being done to solve this problem? What is the relationship between drugs and crime? What is the physiological basis for the power drugs can hold over us? These are but a few of the issues explored in this far-ranging series.

Educating people about the dangers of drugs can go a long way towards minimizing the desperate consequences of substance abuse for individuals and society as a whole. Luckily, human beings have the resources to solve even the most serious problems that beset them, once they make the commitment to do so. As one keen and sensitive observer, Dr. Lewis Thomas, has said,

> There is nothing at all absurd about the human condition. We matter. It seems to me a good guess, hazarded by a good many people who have thought about it, that we may be engaged in the formation of something like a mind for the life of this planet. If this is so, we are still at the most primitive stage, still fumbling with language and thinking, but infinitely capacitated for the future. Looked at this way, it is remarkable that we've come as far as we have in so short a period, really no time at all as geologists measure time. We are the newest, youngest, and the brightest thing around.

DRUGS
&
CIVILIZATION

The ruins of Machu Picchu, a fortress city of the Incas located in the Peruvian Andes. The Incas regarded coca as sacred and incorporated its use into their religious rituals.

AUTHOR'S PREFACE

> Soon her eye fell on a little glass box that was lying under the table: she opened it, and found in it a very small cake, on which the words "eat me" were beautifully marked in currants. "Well, I'll eat it," said Alice, "and if it makes me grow larger, I can reach the key; and if it makes me grow smaller, I can creep under the door; so either way I'll get into the garden, and I don't care which happens!"
>
> *Lewis Carroll,* Alice in Wonderland

Since the dawn of civilization, people have sampled just about every imaginable natural food or drink. Like Alice, humans discovered very early on that many edible substances have mysterious, mind-altering properties. Furthermore, humans have learned how to manufacture drugs, many of which are also psychoactive. Some drugs soothe or stimulate, relieve pain, prevent or cure disease, produce feelings of well being or induce sleep. Others cause hallucinations, coma, even death. Alice's system of learning about her "very small cake" is appropriate only in Wonderland. In real life such casual experimentation can be dangerous and even fatal.

But no matter the risks, the history of drug use dates back at least 10 thousand years. The discovery that a combination of grain, fruit or berries, and water will ferment in a warm temperature, thus yielding an intoxicating potion, was probably made during the Stone Age. A modern parallel may be found in the cultures of primitive peoples. Anthropologists have noted that most of them have learned, by a process of trial and error, that chewing, sucking, or inhaling the leaves, fruits, or roots of certain plants will bring about changes in their physical and psychological states. Alcohol is the substance most widely used by primitive tribes to attain such states.

Recently, some anthropologists have speculated that the discovery of grain-derived alcohol, particularly beer, may have given wandering hunter-gatherer tribes of the Old Stone Age the incentive to settle down in villages to pursue agriculture, thus ensuring a constant grain supply.

Drug use is woven into the history of civilization. People have used drugs for pleasure, social interaction, medicine, rebellion, self-exploration, creativity, religious ceremonies, and as commodities in economic trade. At one time or another, various cultures have considered certain drugs as sacred because of their function in religious observances, and regarded other drugs as evil and to be avoided. (Because psychoactive drugs affect moods and states of consciousness, it is probably the state of mind or mood that is approved or disapproved of, rather than the drug itself.)

The Incas, a Peruvian Indian tribe that achieved a high degree of civilization between 1200 and 1533 C.E., regarded coca as sacred. After the Spanish conquest of South America in the mid-16th century, coca was condemned as diabolical by the Catholic church, which deemed only Christian saints, relics, and sacraments as sacred. The church also considered coffee to be a tool of the devil when it was introduced to Europe in the 17th century, because the Church regarded anything that came from the East to be wicked. In Arabia, however, Muslims had been using coffee in religious ceremonies for 800 years.

In different cultures during different historical periods, drugs have been exalted and condemned, feared and revered. Heroin, once regarded as a miracle drug and widely prescribed and used during the 19th century, is now recognized as a menace to health and society. Alcohol, the most popular drug in the United States and Europe, was prohibited in this country from 1920 to 1933. When tobacco was first introduced into Europe, an immediate antipathy developed toward smoking. Tobacco use was prohibited and, in some countries, punishable by death. Later, England established the colony of Virginia in the New World for the express purpose of growing tobacco. Hemp, the source of rope and paint oil as well as marijuana and hashish, was also grown in colonial America. Entries in George Washington's journal indicate that the father of our country was familiar with *all* the uses of hemp.

Cultural uses of drugs also vary. Some cultures use them only occasionally for medicinal and ceremonial purposes; others have no restrictions on their use. Although it has not been determined why some people tend to use drugs abusively, it has been suggested that cultures in which a drug has been used moderately over the course of many centuries

A five-dollar bill printed in 1778 in colonial Virginia, decorated with crossed tobacco leaves. This colony was established by the British for the express purpose of growing tobacco.

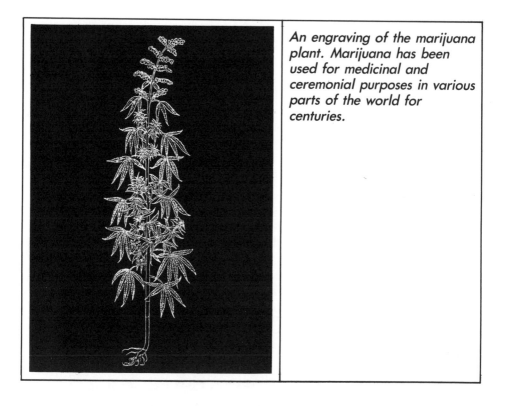

An engraving of the marijuana plant. Marijuana has been used for medicinal and ceremonial purposes in various parts of the world for centuries.

seem to have fewer incidents of adverse drug reactions and addictions, possibly because of genetic adaptations.

There is also a wide cultural variation in the forms in which a drug is taken. This, in turn, determines the potency of the dose and the way it affects the user. In general, a drug that is refined (and hence very concentrated) and then injected directly into the bloodstream has a more powerful and immediate effect than a drug in its natural form taken orally.

The individual drug experience also varies from one person to the next. Differences in individual body chemistry result in varying sensitivities to any given drug. A cup of coffee containing the same amount of caffeine may be relaxing for one person, stimulating to another, and bring on an attack of "coffee nerves" in a third. Individual body chemistry also fluctuates, so that a dose of a drug taken in the morning may have a different effect from that of the same dose taken in the afternoon or evening.

People also have varying degrees of tolerance to a drug. A person who habitually uses a drug builds up a tolerance to it after a period of time and may need a higher dose to achieve the original effect. A confirmed coffee drinker may need two or three cups to feel alert, whereas someone who is not accustomed to drinking coffee may feel a "buzz" for several hours after drinking only one cup.

The dose, or amount, of a drug taken also determines its effect. This is fairly obvious to anyone who has attended a gathering where alcoholic drinks are served. After one or two drinks, most people are relaxed and sociable; after several more, they may become extremely intoxicated. Very large amounts of alcohol are toxic and can even cause death, especially if the user is not accustomed to drinking alcohol.

Body chemistry, tolerance, the purity and size of a dose, and the method of ingestion are classified as pharmacological

A pipe used for smoking crack, a concentrated and highly addictive form of cocaine. The form in which a drug is taken influences the effect it has on each individual user.

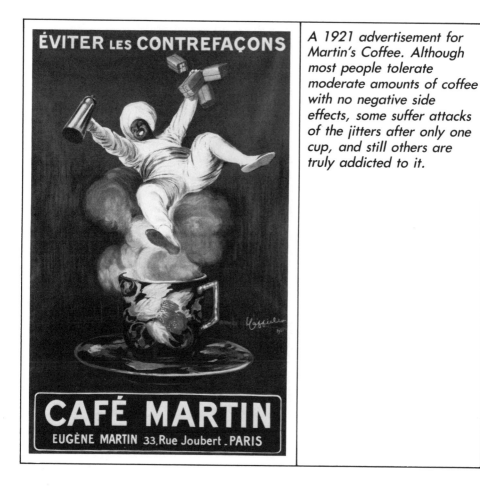

A 1921 advertisement for Martin's Coffee. Although most people tolerate moderate amounts of coffee with no negative side effects, some suffer attacks of the jitters after only one cup, and still others are truly addicted to it.

factors that influence the effect of a drug. Psychological and sociological factors, or the relationship that an individual or a society has to a drug, are equally important. These are known as the *set* and *setting*.

The set is the frame of mind in which a person or a group comes to a drug experience and the expectations they bring with them. A hospital patient who takes cocaine or morphine to relieve pain will have a different experience from that of someone who takes either of these drugs for "kicks." A person who is tense or fearful about using a drug will probably have a different experience from that of one who is confident and relaxed. This is particularly true in the case of hallucinogens, such as LSD, mescaline, and marijuana.

The setting in which a drug is taken also influences the experience. The setting is the physical and psychological environment in which the drug is taken: with friends or with strangers, in a home or in a place of worship or hospital, in a culture that approves or discourages use of that particular drug.

In *Drugs and Civilization*, we will explore some of the sets and settings in which people have used drugs. Through the ages, these have made up a colorful and sometimes tragic and violent chapter in our social history.

A statue of a poppy goddess from ancient Crete. The ancient Greeks incorporated opium, the psychoactive drug derived from poppy plants, into their mythology and religious rituals.

CHAPTER 1

DRUGS, MAGIC, AND RELIGION

Insofar as he transcends his ordinary self and his ordinary mode of awareness, the mystic is able to enlarge his vision to look more deeply into the unfathomable miracle of existence.
Aldous Huxley, "The Drugs That Shape Men's Minds"

Throughout history, people have sought to transcend, or go beyond the limits of, their ordinary experience of the world by attaining altered states of consciousness. Their search for mystic communion with their diety, or dieties, has taken diverse forms.

The art and architecture of churches and temples and the incense and music of various liturgies combine to create a joyful or solemn mood and induce feelings of transcendence, in which everyday concerns are temporarily forgotten and the mind defers to matters of the spirit. Religious ceremonies in many parts of the world also incorporate such self-hypnosis techniques as continuous dancing, whirling, chanting, rolling, shaking, or drumming to bring the worshipers to trancelike states in which they feel closer to God and one another.

Other ancient practices were attempts to heighten sensory perception by altering body chemistry through fasting. The African Zulus have a saying: "The continually stuffed body cannot see secret things." Cultures in Africa, Australia, and

An 1873 engraving of a Shaker meeting. A sect that originated in 18th-century England, the Shakers danced with shaking movements during religious ceremonies to achieve altered states of consciousness.

North and South America all have depended on fasting to achieve visionary states. So, too, have Hindu yogis and Christian mystics.

Fasting brings about changes in blood-sugar levels, which can drop drastically and cause dizziness or fainting. Spiritual exercises such as the breathing techniques used in yoga and the meditation practices of the Hindu and Buddhist religions also alter consciousness by raising the carbon-dioxide level in the blood, thus inducing deep relaxation, and even sleep.

However, the most widespread means by which individuals and groups have sought to induce visions is the use of psychoactive substances found in nature. Plants, mushrooms, snake venom, or toad skins containing mind-altering chemicals can be found in just about every part of the world. The root of the *iboga plant* is used in religious ceremonies by certain religious cults in the Congo and parts of West Africa. Colombian Indians drink a beverage made from a vine called *yage*. Indians in southern Mexico eat morning glory seeds, and peoples in both North and South America chew — or drink tea brewed from — the dried, round "buttons" of the peyote cactus, which contains mescaline.

All these natural drugs are hallucinogens. To a person under the influence of one of these substances, colors seem very bright, and objects seem to throb or pulse with light and energy. Many cultures that practice drug use for religious reasons hold the belief that such drugs induce an altered state of consciousness, heightening the level of receptivity to portents from their gods — portents that can be interpreted and used for healing the sick and predicting the future.

It is likely that psychoactive drugs were first used for religious purposes among cultures that practiced shamanism, in which priests or priestesses were believed to have the power to communicate with the world of spirits while in a visionary state. The shamans were specialists in sacred mat-

A Navajo medicine man performs a healing chant over a mother and her infant. Medicine men are spiritual leaders as well as healers.

ters, creators of ecstasy, and repositories of ancient knowledge. They were also physicians and sorcerers and thus popularly came to be called "witch doctors," or "medicine men."

Shamanism is still a vital force in many cultures around the world — it is found among the Eskimos, some North and South American Indians, the Siberians, the South Sea Islanders, and various religious sects in Southeast Asia.

The Sacred Mushroom

For millennia, indigenous peoples of both the Old World and North America have idolized psychoactive plants, especially psychedelic mushrooms. *Soma*, for example, is a mysterious plant deity celebrated by the ancient Hindus in the *Rig Veda*, the great Sanskrit epic of the 2nd millennium B.C.E. Many anthropologists believe that Soma is the psychoactive mushroom fly agaric, *A. muscaria*. The fly agaric was also the focus of a Bronze Age sun cult in Scandinavia. Indians in pre-Columbian Mexico carved stone idols of mushrooms 2,500 years ago. *The Codex Vienna* — one of the few pre-Columbian pictorial manuscripts to survive the ravages of the Spanish conquest of Mexico in the 16th century — identifies the sacred mushrooms as female earth deities and credits the gods themselves with establishing the ritual of their use. Spanish priests, after converting the Indians to Christianity, tried unsuccessfully to discourage the use of mushrooms in their converts' religious life. Well into the 20th century, the Laplanders in northern Finland and the tribal peoples of Siberia, especially the shamans, continued to use these fungi to attain states of divine inebriation and inspiration.

The Gift of Prophecy

Ancient Persians, Egyptians, and Greeks ascribed to their priests and priestesses the gift of prophecy, believing that these sacred leaders, while in trancelike states, could foretell the future. The techniques used by these religious leaders to achieve altered states of consciousness were similar to those of the shaman and included fasting, meditation, self-hypnotic ritual, and use of psychoactive drugs. Oldest of all cultivated psychoactive plants is the opium poppy. Among the remains

A detail from a 400 B.C.E. Greek vase depicts a visit to the Oracle of Delphi. Greek oracles often prophesied while in drug-induced states.

of the Minoan (Cretan) and Mycenaean (Greek) civilizations, which flourished from 3000 and 1600 to 1000 B.C.E. respectively, are sculptures of priestesses and goddesses crowned with opium poppies.

The Rites of Ancient Greece

The ancient Greeks incorporated opium into their mythology and religious mysteries, both magical and sacred. They established sacred shrines consecrated to the worship of gods whose divine will might be known in advance. The people would consult priests and priestesses who, acting as intermediaries, would then prophesy, often in the form of enigmatic statements or allegories. As an aid to their communication with divine powers, these religious figures probably burned laurel leaves (bay leaves), poisonous henbane, or marijuana to attain the heightened consciousness necessary for the release of their alleged prophetic powers. (The shrines, the prophets, and the "messages" themselves are all referred to as "oracles.") Ambrosia, "the food of the gods," was wine spiked with intoxicating plants, one of which was probably opium.

Numerous psychoactive plants are native to Greece. Around 800 B.C.E., mushrooms were also known as the "food of the gods," and certain varieties that grew on oak trees supposedly enabled their users to see into the future.

31

A Greek bell-krater — a vase for mixing wine and water — depicts a scene of Persephone rising from the earth in the presence of Hermes, Hecate, and Demeter. The vessel dates from about 440 B.C.E.

The Greeks also made wine from the grapes they culti-vated, which they drank in celebrations honoring the god of fertility, Dionysus. Extreme drunkenness was considered "di-vine ecstasy," the proper state in which to experience the presence of the fertility god in sacred rites symbolizing his death and resurrection. The wine imbibed at these cere-monies was undiluted. At the dinner table, however, it was customary to dilute wine with water.

Plays and poems that have survived from that time also suggest that hallucinogenic herbs were sometimes added to wine. In the epic adventure story the *Odyssey*, the poet Ho-mer relates how Helen of Troy gives the potion *nepenthe* to the Greek hero Odysseus, his son, and companions to lull their grief and pain. Some scholars think nepenthe was wine to which opium, mandrake, henbane, belladonna (deadly nightshade), and possibly marijuana had been added. (Man-drake, henbane, and belladonna all contain powerful hallu-cinogens—and all can be deadly poisons.)

From the 2nd century B.C.E. until the 4th century C.E., secret societies in the Greek cities Athens and Eleusis cele-brated the rites of spring to commemorate the return of the goddess Persephone from Hades, the underworld of Greek mythology. During this ceremony, as many as 3,000 people drank a potion called *Kykeon*. This beverage probably contained barley infested with ergot, a grain fungus that has hallucinogenic properties caused by the presence of lysergic acid, later synthesized in the form of LSD. The experience for which the initiates had long and carefully prepared themselves may have indeed been a communal "acid trip" in which they believed they saw a vision of Persephone.

The Witch's Cauldron

In many cultures, intoxicating plants have been associated specifically with women, their "magical" powers held to be the special province of goddesses and priestesses. In China, for example, the mystical philosophy of Taoism links drugs

A late 17th-century engraving from a book on demonology represents a meeting of witches, with demons and enchanted beasts. Witches often used psychoactive plants in their brews.

with women, earth, nature, and the inner self. Indeed, in most societies it has traditionally been women who gathered from the woods and fields and grew in their gardens the plants used in herbal remedies as well as in religion and magic. Perhaps because they offered stiff competition to the male establishment, or simply because their knowledge seemed mysterious, women herbalists were often called witches. Some did practice witchcraft; the standard ingredients of their witches' brews were henbane, belladonna, mandrake, and skins of toads.

Datura, known as jimsonweed in America, was another favorite plant of witches everywhere. Indians of North and South America used it to induce visions or as a love potion (aphrodisiac). Mandrake, so called because the branches from its roots resemble a man's legs, was also named "satan's ap-

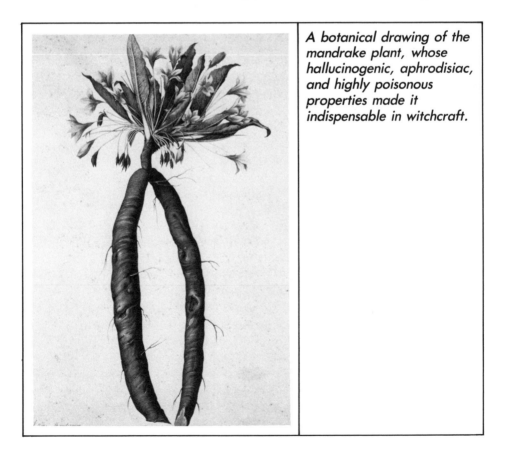

A botanical drawing of the mandrake plant, whose hallucinogenic, aphrodisiac, and highly poisonous properties made it indispensable in witchcraft.

A botanical drawing of the coca plant. Once used in South America as part of spiritual observances, coca is now used by laborers in that part of the world as a palliative against hunger and exhaustion.

ple," at once the most feared component and valued treasure of the witch's garden. It was thought to grow from the seed of a person executed for murder, and according to folklore, the plant shrieked when it was pulled from the ground. Its hallucinogenic, aphrodisiac, and highly poisonous properties made it indispensable to witchcraft. In medicine it was used as an anesthetic, a sedative, and as a remedy for melancholy.

Mama Coca

Coca is a South American plant that is the source of cocaine, one of the world's most powerful stimulants. It was sacred to the Incas, who believed that Mama Coca, as they called cocaine because it was sometimes pictured as a beautiful woman, was associated with the moon goddess. Later, after the Spanish conquest brought Christianity to the New World, Mama Coca was pictured with Jesus and the Virgin Mary.

Incas prayed to Mama Coca before starting journeys. At dangerous points on mountain paths they chewed coca and placed the wad of chewed leaves on stones to appease the gods and prevent injuries. Coca was also used in weddings and initiation rites for young nobles.

Priests used coca along with tobacco to induce a trance that enabled them to see into the future. Before performing religious rituals, they scattered coca leaves as an offering to the gods.

At religious festivals coca was chewed and offered to the goddess of the earth so she would send good harvests. And at funerals the mouth of the corpse was stuffed with coca leaves, and bags of the leaves were placed in the tomb to ease the spirit of the departed into the afterworld.

After the Spanish conquest, the 16th-century Spanish Inquisition, which persecuted those whose beliefs did not conform to Catholic doctrine, tried to put an end to the religious uses of coca as well as to the use of psilocybin mushrooms in Mexican tribal religions.

However, the Spanish conquerors soon discovered that coca had great economic potential. They permitted its use for nonreligious purposes — mainly as a palliative for hunger and the exhaustion that comes from hard labor at high altitudes—but taxed the users.

The Native American Church

One significant, institutionalized use of a hallucinogen in religious rituals involves the Native American Church. Adopted in the mid-1800s by the Kiowa and the Comanche tribes, who live in the United States, this religion, which combines traditional Indian and Christian beliefs, spread to most American Indian tribes between 1880 and 1930. As of 1985 the church had a quarter of a million members.

In the context of their religious observances, members of this group use peyote in nightlong meetings. The ritual begins at sunset and ends at sunrise: Singing, drumming, talking, and ritual cigarette smoking are all part of a ceremony designed to foster a strong bond among worshipers.

When the ceremony starts, a peyote "button" is placed in the center of the crescent-shaped altar that represents the universe. Peyote is handed to the congregation at prescribed intervals. The leader of the meeting, called the "road man," monitors and controls the congregants; no one is allowed to wander away. Members eat breakfast afterward so that the group stays together until the hallucinogenic and unpredictable effects of the drug have worn off.

Church members do not take peyote at these meetings to bring on hallucinations. Rather, it is used to enable members to communicate with one another and with God and to gain insight into themselves and their problems. "Peyote teaches you," the Navahos say. Said one tribe member, "I used to live from day to day, but now I think."

When the Native American Church was established it met with opposition from both the Indian community and law enforcement officials as a result of its drug practices. After a series of legal battles in the late 19th and early 20th centuries, in which the church members maintained they had a constitutional right to practice their religion freely, the use of peyote was finally legally permitted in their religious ceremonies.

Comanche Indians at a peyote ceremony. Some American Indian tribes use peyote as a means of transcending ordinary consciousness in order to commune with the spiritual universe.

Dr. Richard Alpert (left) and Dr. Timothy Leary are reunited in 1983 on the 20th anniversary of their dismissal from the faculty of Harvard University for their use and promotion of psychedelic drugs.

Modern Times: The Search for Spiritual Meaning

In contemporary Western societies, psychoactive drugs do not play much of a role in religious rites and ceremonies. To be sure, wine has symbolic significance in both Jewish and Christian rituals, but it is not used as a means of achieving altered states of consciousness.

In the 1960s and 1970s, some experimentation with LSD was rationalized in the name of spiritual enrichment, but most drug experiences were solipsistic at best, psychologically destructive at worst. Certainly, the ephemeral cult of LSD, heralded by men like former Harvard professor Timothy Leary as a legitimate agent of enlightenment, never developed into anything like a valid form of spiritualism.

As anthropologist Margaret Mead wrote: "It must be recognized that there is no necessary relationship between the use of drugs and religious experience. The ordinary LSD trip has no more necessary relationship to mystical experience than the drinking of ten cocktails has, after which many people experience various alterations of consciousness."

Needless to say, Mead's remarks do not refer to the religious observances of peoples who have incorporated the use of psychoactive plants into ritual. She refers, rather, to those who would confound drug taking with spirituality, with results ranging from self-delusion to self-destruction.

An engraving of a 16th-century pharmacy. The quest for drugs to relieve pain and treat illness is as old as civilization itself.

CHAPTER 2

MEDICINAL USES OF DRUGS

In addition to their roles as spiritual leaders, shamans were physicians, entrusted with both the physical and spiritual health of the tribe. These indigenous peoples seemed to understand a concept that has only recently been rediscovered by modern medical science: Health of the body is linked with health of the spirit. The word *psychosomatic,* referring to a physical symptom that may be caused by psychological distress, comes from the Greek words for body and soul.

It is not surprising, then, that many of the drugs used in medicine are psychoactive, affecting the mind as well as the body. Some are important in surgery and healing because they dull the sense of pain and also induce sleep. This class of drugs is known as depressants and includes the opiates, sedatives, anesthetics, and alcohol.

Before medicine had developed into a modern science where specific remedies were prescribed for specific diseases, the best a physician could do for patients was to reduce their pain and help them to rest so that the natural healing process could take its course. Doctors had to rely on such remedies as psychoactive plants to help ease pain and allow the body to rest. These drugs are now used in ways that are remarkably similar to those of old-fashioned folk medicine.

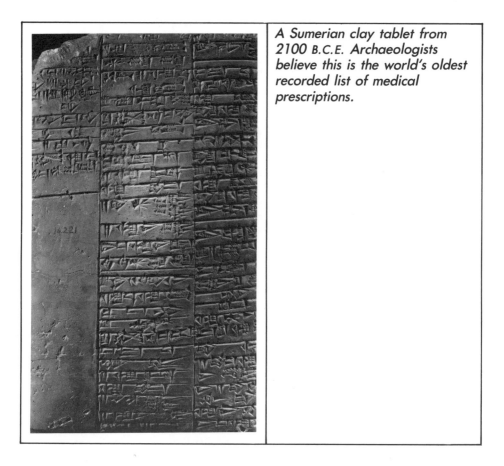

A Sumerian clay tablet from 2100 B.C.E. Archaeologists believe this is the world's oldest recorded list of medical prescriptions.

Opium

Opium has been used for its medicinal properties since ancient times. In the modern era, despite extensive research, no medicine has been found that is as effective as the opiates in relieving extreme pain. Aside from its painkilling properties, opium paralyzes the bowels and is useful in controlling diarrhea. It also depresses the respiratory system and, if taken in proper doses, is an effective cough suppressant. Sadly, opiates are also classic drugs of abuse. They are highly addictive and offer a deceptive, temporary sense of well-being and euphoria that requires larger and larger doses to maintain. Opium addicts who discontinue the drug can suffer painful and very unpleasant withdrawal symptoms.

Opium was first used medicinally during the 6th century B.C.E. in Greece. According to legend, Aesculapius, a mythical healer, restored the hero Hippolytus to life with a "magical simple," a potion made with a single ingredient. Statues of Aesculapius crowned with poppies suggest that the substance he used was probably opium.

Temples were built to honor Aesculapius, and they were presided over by physician-priests. Around 600 B.C.E., when people came to the temple of Aesculapius seeking to be cured of illness, the physicians would first give them opium, which causes vivid dreams. After the patient took the opium, he was led off to sleep. When he woke, he would recount his dreams, and the physician would prescribe remedies on the basis of what those dreams revealed. Although this approach to diagnosis may seem to us like hocus-pocus, it highlights the fact that the Greeks were aware of significant links between mind and body. Relating physical illness to the unconscious was an extraordinarily sophisticated perception for the time.

By the 5th century B.C.E. the Aesculapians were known as the best doctors in Greece. They had a wide knowledge of plants and their uses in healing, and they also practiced surgery. Their approach to health was a sensible regimen of good diet, good sleep habits, and exercise.

A Greek relief from the late 4th or early 5th century B.C.E. shows Aesculapius, a mythical healer, with his daughter Hygeia, the goddess of health. Statues of Aesculapius crowned with poppies indicate that he may have used opium in his healing potions.

Hippocrates, who is known as the father of medicine, was the most renowned of the Aesculapians. He prescribed opium for sleeplessness, internal complaints, women's diseases, epilepsy, and dropsy, which is an accumulation of water in the tissues.

By the second century C.E. the physician Galen, one of the last of the Aesculapians, was prescribing opium for high blood pressure, uncontrollable anger, and cholera, a contagious disease that affects the stomach and intestines.

From the 5th to the 1st century B.C.E., the poppy was used elsewhere in Europe by barber-physicians, midwives, and herbalists who mashed the pods into paste for dressing wounds or brewed them into tea used to treat internal ailments.

In Persia during the early part of the 11th century, the physician Avicenna devised a way of standardizing the amount of opium administered to patients, thus minimizing considerably the risk of overdose. In Europe, the French surgeon Guy de Chauliac, who practiced from 1340 to 1370, gave opium to his patients as a sedative.

A bust of Hippocrates, the Greek physician known as "the father of medicine." Hippocrates prescribed opium for a number of physical ailments.

A detail from a 17th-century Persian miniature shows the 11th-century physician Avicenna surrounded by his students. Avicenna devised a method of standardizing the amount of opium administered to patients.

From the 13th to the 16th centuries, during the Spanish Inquisition, the use of opium even for medicinal purposes was condemned by the Catholic church. The Inquisition was a tribunal set up by the church during the Middle Ages to abolish heresy. All thinking that did not conform to Catholic doctrine was condemned as heresy and sometimes punished by death. Mind-altering substances that might lead the believer from the path of righteousness and correct belief were considered suspect and possibly agents of the devil.

In the early 16th century, Paracelsus, a brilliant and eccentric Swiss physician, restored the use of opium to European medicine. After his death, the poppy was considered a remedy for all illnesses.

In 1680 Thomas Syndenham, an English apothecary, mixed opium with sherry, saffron, cinnamon, and cloves and created the potent laudanum. Syndenham claimed that the alcohol in the sherry purified the opium of its addictive properties.

FAMOSO·DOCTOR PARESELSVS

An oil portrait of Paracelsus, the 16th-century physician who reintroduced the use of opium to Western medicine.

This laudanum, believed to be a "safe" form of opium, was soon an ingredient of patent medicines. By 1700 no fewer than four brands of patent medicines containing laudanum were on the market. Until the mid-1800s, these medicines continued to be popular treatments for coughs, headache, toothache, menstrual pain, depression, nervousness, and insomnia, and were taken as well for recreational purposes.

In 1805 Frederic Serturner, then a German pharmacist's apprentice, made a discovery that was to revolutionize medicine and relieve physical and mental suffering for the next century. In trying to isolate the single active ingredient of the juice of the opium poppy, he dissolved the opium in acid so that crystals were formed. Then he washed the crystals in a solution of alcohol and ammonia. The result was a gray powder that he called morphine, after Morpheus, the Greek god of sleep.

In 1817 Serturner's discovery was announced in medical journals. Some of the leading pharmaceutical houses — Merck, Sharpe & Dohme, among others — began manufacturing morphine, and its use quickly spread.

The hypodermic needle was invented in 1843. That same year, Alexander Wood, an English surgeon, experimented with injecting morphine under the skin. He discovered that when injected, the drug quickly entered the bloodstream and was three times more powerful than when taken orally.

Morphine became the miracle drug of the 19th century and was affectionately referred to as "God's own medicine." Soldiers fighting in the American Civil War were given morphine not only to soothe the pain of their injuries but also to relieve the symptoms of dysentery, a gastrointestinal disease that plagued soldiers on both sides. Shortly after the war, however, it was discovered that the drug had an undesirable side effect. Many of the soldiers who had been given morphine came home dependent on it. So many soldiers were addicted, in fact, that their affliction became known as the "soldier's disease."

Frederic Serturner (left) and Alexander Wood. Serturner synthesized morphine from opium in 1805. In 1843 Wood discovered that morphine reached the bloodstream most quickly when injected under the skin.

In 1898 the Bayer Company in Germany developed yet another opium derivative, 10 times more powerful than morphine. Like opium and morphine before it, this new drug was hailed as a wonder drug and was indeed highly effective in relieving coughs and colds, bronchitis, emphysema, asthma, and tuberculosis. It was also used to treat morphine addiction. To suggest the heroic curative power of this new drug, its creators named it heroin.

It soon became apparent that heroin, too, was highly addictive. By 1919 no fewer than a quarter of a million, and perhaps as many as 1 million people in America alone, were addicted to heroin or some other form of opium. In fact, during the late 19th and early 20th centuries, patent medicines that purported to treat a range of ailments were routinely laced with opiates, cocaine, or alcohol.

A 19th-century poster for McMunn's Elixir of Opium. During the late 19th and early 20th centuries many patent medicines contained opiates, and addiction to these dangerous drugs was rampant.

As the dangerous addictive properties of the opiates became more apparent, the U.S. government started to issue legislation controlling the use of these drugs. The first of these, the Pure Food and Drug Act, was passed in 1906 and ordered the contents of over-the-counter medications to be carefully monitored. Another step toward regulating the rampant use of narcotics was taken in 1914 when Congress passed the Harrison Act. It required every doctor to have a license number to prescribe a narcotic and every pharmacist to obtain the number before filling the prescription. This system remains in place today, and the use of opiates is rigidly controlled throughout the medical profession.

Cocaine

Much like the opiates, cocaine has both therapeutic properties and a high potential for addiction. A stimulant, cocaine can initially improve alertness and performance, and the numbing power of the drug has also made it a useful topical anesthetic. But the bad effects of cocaine far outweigh the good; its initial stimulating effects can be deceiving. Long-term users have to take the drug in increasing quantities in order to experience the pleasurable effects, and high doses of the drug can lead to brain damage and death.

The leaves of the coca plant, *erythroxylon coca*, have been used for hundreds of years by the Indians of South America. They chewed the leaves for energy and endurance, to gain a sense of well-being, and to allay their hunger. They also used coca leaves in folk remedies for stomach upsets, diarrhea, cramps, and nausea. Tea was made from the leaves and used to treat rheumatism, asthma, and malaria. Juice made from the leaves was used to soothe sore throats and eye irritations and as a local anesthetic in surgery.

Coca was introduced into Europe in the 1600s by the returning Spanish conquerers of South America. But it was not until various German chemists isolated cocaine from the coca leaf between 1855 and 1862 that anyone in Europe or the United States paid much attention to this psychoactive plant. By the 1870s and 1880s this indifference had vanished, replaced by a virtual euphoria over the purported healing powers of the new drug. It was mixed with wine to make a concoction called Vin Mariani, and doctors throughout Europe began recommending it to their patients for sore throats. Military physicians also expressed interest in cocaine's ability to enable armies to walk long distances without food or sleep. A British medical journal editorialized in 1876 that coca would be a "new stimulant and a new narcotic: two forms of novelty in excitement which our modern civilization is highly likely to esteem."

Ironically, cocaine was very quickly hailed by many influential physicians as a cure for addiction to morphine, opium, and alcohol. In 1884 two events focused further attention on cocaine. The first was the publication of Sigmund Freud's article titled "Über Coca" ("On Cocaine"). In it, Freud, the founder of psychoanalysis, recommended coca or cocaine for a variety of illnesses and described his own use of the drug, which he apparently took orally with some reg-

Sigmund Freud, the father of psychoanalysis. In 1884, Freud published Über Coca, an essay that championed the use of cocaine, claiming that it produced "exhilaration and lasting euphoria."

A Greek immigrant stands outside his turn-of-the-century pharmacy. Window displays advertise dyes, root beer, castor oil, homeopathic medicines — and cocaine.

ularity. His enthusiasm for the drug was boundless, and he wrote that it produced "exhilaration and lasting euphoria." "Über Coca" influenced many otherwise doubtful physicians and prompted Parke-Davis and other drug companies to advertise cocaine as "the most important therapeutic discovery of the age."

The second major event of 1884 concerning cocaine was the discovery by Carl Koller, a colleague of Freud, of the drug's usefulness as a topical anesthetic in eye surgery. Although cocaine anesthesia was at that time unpredictable, it inspired further research. In the same year William Halsted of the Johns Hopkins University School of Medicine in Baltimore invented nerve block, a way of deadening isolated sections of the body by injecting cocaine into nerves. Spinal anesthesia through administration of cocaine was introduced in 1898. The following year saw the invention of novocaine, a synthetic substitute for cocaine without toxic side effects.

Gradually, however, evidence of cocaine's limitations and drawbacks began to mount, and its medical importance waned. Along with opium, the use of cocaine in patent medicines was controlled by the Harrison Act of 1914. Though the negative effects of this drug have been evident for close to a century now, the history of efforts to control its abuse is still being written in the 1980s.

Amphetamine

Like cocaine, amphetamine is a stimulant that speeds up the passing of electrical impulses through the nervous system so that people who use it experience heightened alertness and powers of concentration and increased intellectual and physical endurance. Amphetamine also suppresses the appetite, as cocaine does, and was once prescribed for weight control. Interestingly, amphetamine has a calming effect on children who are hyperactive and unable to settle down to concentrate. Occasional low doses of amphetamine do not usually create dependencies or personality changes. The effects of heavy, chronic amphetamine abuse, however, are similar to those of cocaine. Users experience irregular heartbeat, dizziness, and anxiety and suffer such effects as fatigue and depression when the drug is withdrawn. Some people become psychotic after prolonged, heavy abuse.

Because amphetamine is a synthetic (i.e., manufactured) drug, it does not have the long history of medicinal use that organic drugs have. Originally synthesized in 1887 by a German scientist, amphetamine was not marketed until 1932, when it was discovered that the drug could treat nasal congestion by shrinking the mucous membranes of the nose. Three years later pharmacists recognized the stimulating effects of amphetamine, and the American Medical Association approved the use of the drug for such disorders as narcolepsy (uncontrollable sleepiness). In fact, between 1932 and 1946 the pharmaceutical industry promoted 39 different clinical uses for amphetamine. Wrongly included on the list were treatment for schizophrenia (it was found that amphetamine abuse can in fact cause symptoms similar to those of schizophrenia) and opiate addiction. It was also believed during this time that amphetamine was not addictive.

In the 1950s amphetamine was being tested as a possible treatment for depression and was widely prescribed as an appetite suppressant. In addition, people who had to stay awake for long hours, such as college students and truck drivers, began using the drug for its stimulating effects. Recreational use and abuse of amphetamine reached a peak in the 1960s, when hard-core users began injecting the drug intravenously to get a quicker and more intense effect.

Since that time, medical use of amphetamine has waned considerably as knowledge about its several negative side effects has accumulated. Scientific studies have shown that long-term use of amphetamine can lead to addiction and cause psychosis. Most doctors no longer recommend amphetamine as an appetite suppressant, and the drug is now most commonly prescribed as a treatment for narcolepsy.

Alcohol

In general, alcohol is regarded as a recreational drug. It does not have, as opium or cocaine does, specific pain-numbing properties. However, it has been used for therapeutic purposes for centuries. Although liquor was probably originally distilled in the Greco-Roman era, it was rediscovered in Europe in 1250. Following this development, drinking spirits became associated with medicinal customs and were sold as medicines by monks, physicians, and apothecaries. During this time Arnau de Villanova, a professor of medicine who taught in France, called distilled spirits *aqua vitae* (water of life) because it "strengthens the body and prolongs life." Indeed, alcohol was used in the Middle Ages as a medicine for the plague, an analgesic for pain, and a cold preventive in damp and cold climates. Alcohol continues to be used for therapeutic purposes in some European countries, such as Italy and France.

Alcohol has also been used for medicinal purposes in the United States. During the 1800s, for example, the early American settlers used alcohol as a painkiller when anesthetics or opiates were not available. Alcohol was also used as a substitute for anesthetics in procedures ranging from tooth extractions to amputation. Until Prohibition went into effect in 1920, American hospital pharmacies were stocked with whiskey and several varieties of wine. The wines were alternately prescribed as appetite stimulants, sedatives, and treatments for fevers and nervous ailments. Alcohol was also prescribed as a diuretic, a substance that causes the body to lose excess water. Even in the late 20th century, many people use alcohol for the specific purpose of calming their nerves or getting to sleep. The popular "hot toddy," made with whiskey, lemon juice, and hot water, is often recommended for treatment of a mild cold.

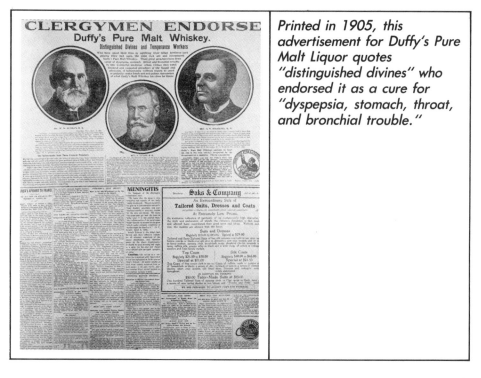

Printed in 1905, this advertisement for Duffy's Pure Malt Liquor quotes "distinguished divines" who endorsed it as a cure for "dyspepsia, stomach, throat, and bronchial trouble."

Alcohol is not harmful if used occasionally and in moderation. However, people who habitually use the drug, whether for recreational or medicinal purposes, may become physically and psychologically dependent. Moderate intake of alcohol can cause slurred speech, delayed reaction, and lack of physical coordination; large doses and prolonged use can cause "blackout," in which a person can neither control nor remember his or her actions. In very large doses, alcohol can cause coma or even death. Chronic use of the drug can severely damage the liver, brain, and central nervous system. Abrupt withdrawal from a drinking habit can result in a condition known as *delirium tremens*, or DTs, characterized by hallucinations, trembling, or convulsions and in some cases may be fatal. Certainly, the dangers of prolonged alcohol use far outweigh the marginal medicinal benefits.

Barbiturates

Barbiturates are currently prescribed for many of the conditions that used to be treated by alcohol and the opiates. They slow down vital body functions tied to the central nervous system and are used to induce sleep and reduce levels of anxiety and tension.

Throughout history, people have looked for the ideal remedy to problems of sleeplessness or stress. Opiates, alcohol, and potions containing mandrake and other herbs were tried and rejected in turn. Chloral hydrate, a white powder used as an anesthetic and sedative, was prescribed for insomnia and to calm restless and manic patients in asylums. For a time, middle-class women employed it to combat stress, but because of its unpleasant effects and foul taste and odor, it was supplanted by other drugs.

It was against this background that barbiturates were introduced. In 1903 two German scientists who were experimenting with the chemical compound barbituric acid invented a new chemical they called barbital. Small doses of the drug appeared to calm the nerves, and moderate doses proved to be an effective sleeping aid.

Barbital was introduced on the market under the trade name Veronal and was only the first of dozens of such compounds. Eventually, 50 different brands of barbiturates were approved for medical use.

Barbiturates can be short-, intermediate-, or long-acting, depending upon how quickly the drugs take effect and how long they last. The short- and intermediate-acting barbiturates are used most often as sedatives and tranquilizers. Long-acting barbiturates are used most successfully to control certain types of epileptic seizures.

But for each of the barbiturates' beneficial properties, there is also a harmful side effect. The margin between a safe barbiturates dose and an overdose is narrow. Barbiturate overdose results in a state of anesthesia accompanied by general depression to the central nervous system. Breathing is slowed, body temperature drops, the heartbeat slows, and blood pressure falls. This may lead to coma and even death.

Shortly after the drugs were introduced, reports of fatal poisoning by barbiturates began to surface. As use of the drugs grew, so did the number of deaths attributed to them. In some countries, barbiturates were the cause of more deaths than any other compound. During the mid-1950s, for example, 70% of all admissions at one poison treatment center were due to barbiturate overdose.

Tranquilizers

Once the dangerous side effects of barbiturates, including their highly addictive properties, were recognized, scientists began searching for safer alternatives for anxiety and insomnia relief. In the 1950s tranquilizers were developed.

Tranquilizers fall into two different categories: major and minor. Major tranquilizers, such as Thorazine, are used to treat major psychiatric illnesses and are administered under close medical supervision. Minor tranquilizers, such as Valium and Librium, are used to treat neurotic conditions and temporary anxiety. They are generally considered by the public to be safe, nonaddictive antidotes to stress.

Valium and Librium are the two best-known tranquilizers today and rank, respectively, as the two most widely prescribed drugs in the world. Their reputation as harmless substances has been slightly tarnished, however. It has been discovered that tranquilizers resemble barbiturates in a number of ways. They can cause feelings of drunkenness, can be addictive, and have been known to cause delirium tremens during withdrawal. To be sure, the overdose potential of Valium and Librium is much lower than that of the barbiturates. Also, despite some serious incidences of abuse, these drugs are not as inherently dangerous as the barbiturates. Nonetheless, when combined with alcohol, tranquilizers, like barbiturates, can be deadly.

LSD and Other Hallucinogens

LSD is a chemical derivative of ergot, a fungus that infects barley and other grains. It is known as a hallucinogen, or psychedelic drug, because of its mind-altering properties.

The chemical compound for LSD was isolated in 1938 by the Swiss chemist Dr. Albert Hofmann. Five years later, Hofman accidentally ingested a tiny dose of the drug and described the experience as a "not unpleasant delirium characterized by excited fantasies." A week later, after having taken a second dose of LSD, he reported that he experienced "visual disturbances ... the faces around me appeared as grotesque, colored masks."

Since that time, psychiatrists and psychologists have repeatedly conducted their own experiments with LSD in at-

Dr. Albert Hofmann, who isolated LSD from ergot in 1938.

tempts to learn more about the workings of the human mind. Studies concluded that the drug altered normal thought processes and undermined the powers of logic and reason.

Because it was believed that the thought of LSD users resembled the thoughts of the mentally ill — specifically schizophrenics — psychiatrists and other mental health professionals began to administer it to themselves. By experiencing drug-induced mental states that approximated schizophrenia, during the 1950s, they hoped to gain a better understanding of the nature of this and other mental illnesses. LSD was also given to patients undergoing psychotherapy in order to help them gain personal insights and remember events in their past that may have contributed to their illness. The drug was also used unsuccessfully to treat alcoholism and to help terminal cancer patients come to terms with their illness.

When LSD was not available, mescaline and psilocybin, two hallucinogenic substances derived from the peyote cactus and certain species of mushrooms, respectively, were used for similar purposes in psychotherapy.

In the 1980s a few psychiatrists continue to use LSD in controlled settings as a treatment for severe forms of mental illness, such as schizophrenia. For the most part, though, legally synthesized LSD is unavailable even to scientific researchers. The medicinal use of this and other hallucinogens is virtually at a standstill.

Marijuana

Marijuana is derived from the hemp plant, *cannabis sativa*. Though its use in the United States is primarily a 20th-century phenomenon, it has been used as an intoxicant in various parts of the world for centuries.

Marijuana was first described in print in a Chinese book of medicine in the second century B.C.E. and was used in China as an anesthetic 5,000 years ago. The ancient Persians, Greeks, Romans, East Indians, and Assyrians used the drug to control muscle spasm, to reduce pain, and to treat indigestion. It has since been used as an herbal preparation in the folk medicine of Asia and Africa. The Assyrians also grew it for use as incense in the 9th century.

As early as 1611 marijuana was cultivated for its fiber in colonial Jamestown, Virginia. Marijuana was also used in Western medical practices. In the 19th century it was used in America by the medical profession for treating ailments such as spastic condition, headaches, labor pains, insomnia, and menstrual cramps. In fact, in the last half of the 19th century the American medical journals published more than 100 articles that discussed the use of marijuana for various medical purposes. From 1870 until 1941 it was listed in the *U.S. Pharmacopeia* as a useful medicine. Drug companies manufactured various preparations of cannabis such as extracts, tinctures, and herbal packages, which were available in any pharmacy. In 1941, however, it was dropped from the two main professional directories of drugs in the United States. It continues to be used medicinally in the Middle East and Asia.

It is known that marijuana is harmful to one's physical health. Carcinogens in marijuana smoke enter directly into the lungs and spread to other organs and tissues. Just as exposure over time to the toxic drug nicotine in cigarettes may be hazardous to one's health, long-term use of marijuana can cause cancer or other lung diseases, such as emphysema.

Nonetheless, some doctors believe that marijuana is an excellent remedy for some ailments, particularly as a relief from the nausea and vomiting induced by the chemotherapy that certain cancer patients undergo. Some experts also maintain that marijuana is useful in the treatment of glaucoma, an eye disease that causes blindness. In the 1980s, however, these medicinal uses of marijuana are outlawed in most parts of the United States.

General Anesthetics

General anesthetics are used in surgery because of their ability to depress a patient's central nervous system and bring on a temporary insensitivity to pain. Three of these substances are ether, chloroform, and nitrous oxide. The first two are vaporized liquids that cause unconsciousness when inhaled. Nitrous oxide is a weaker drug but does have pain-reducing properties. All three drugs have served as vital pain-killers during medical procedures and are, for that reason, major discoveries. Because they induce giddiness and temporary hilarity, however, all can be drugs of abuse and are potentially addictive.

Ether is a distilled mixture of alcohol and sulfuric acid. There is evidence that it was discovered as early as 1540, but for centuries thereafter it was used mostly for amusement — anesthetized actors and participants behaved comically and without inhibition during staged performances — and occasionally as a treatment for respiratory illness. In the 1700s, some doctors prescribed ether in liquid form as a tonic and pain reliever. But ether continued to be largely used for recreational purposes until William T. G. Morton, a Boston dentist, finally employed it as an agent of painless surgery during a tooth extraction he performed at Massachusetts General Hospital in 1846.

Chloroform, which was first used in Germany, France, and the United States in the 1840s, has a similar history. Like ether, it was first used for recreational purposes and was inhaled for its mildly hallucinogenic effects. In 1847 James T. Simpson, a Scottish physician, introduced this gas as an anesthetic in surgery and childbirth. His most famous patient was Queen Victoria, whom Dr. Simpson treated with chloroform to ease the delivery of her eighth child. Because chloroform is highly flammable it is no longer used in surgery.

A physician administers nitrous oxide to a patient during the 1880s. Inhalant anesthetics were essential medical discoveries, but many of the compounds used were also subject to abuse.

Nitrous oxide, popularly known as "laughing gas," was a third drug initially used for recreational purposes. This anesthetic was discovered in 1772 by Sir Joseph Priestley, an English physician. But Horace Wells, a Boston physician, was the first person to introduce the drug to the medical establishment.

In 1844, Wells performed a painless tooth extraction using nitrous oxide. A year later, he tried to demonstrate this technique again, before a Harvard Medical School class. This patient shrieked in agony, and Wells was humiliated.

William Morton, a colleague of Wells, is generally credited with refining the use of nitrous oxide and other anesthetic gases in surgery. As mentioned earlier, nitrous oxide is not as strong as ether or chloroform and does not produce unconsciousness. It is used most commonly for its pain-reducing properties in dental procedures and in childbirth, and as a sedative preceding the administration of a stronger general anesthetic in surgery.

In order to be effective medical drugs, general anesthetics must be administered under careful supervision. Long-term recreational use of these drugs can damage the heart, kidneys, liver, and other vital body parts. Even a single overdose can cause psychosis, brain damage, coma, or death.

The Double-Edged Sword

In large part, the history of medicine is the history of pharmacology. The discovery and refinement of medicines — from such relatively primitive painkillers as whiskey to the complex synthetic drugs now being used to treat a range of mental and physical illnesses — are among the triumphs of human civilization. But as each new substance is ushered in, it may carry with it not only inherently negative side effects but also the potential for abuse.

A self-portrait of the 19th-century poet Baudelaire smoking marijuana. Like many artists and writers during this period, Baudelaire experimented with the mind-expanding potential of drugs.

CHAPTER 3

DRUGS AND CREATIVITY

Weave a circle round him thrice, And close your eyes with
holy dread, For he on honey-dew hath fed, And drunk the milk
of Paradise

Samuel Taylor Coleridge, "Kubla Khan"

Although there is no evidence that creative people take
drugs more often than other people, drug use by writers,
artists, and performers is more visible. The list of writers who
have recorded drinking and drug-taking experiences is a very
long one, beginning with the Greek poet Homer's references
to wine in about 800 B.C.E., and brought up to date regularly
in modern best-sellers. The first known woman writer, the
Greek poet Sappho (fl.c. 620–c.565 B.C.E.), shows some fa-
miliarity with opium. The Roman poets Virgil and Ovid,
France's Rabelais and Spain's Cervantes all wrote of wine. In
1821 the English writer Thomas De Quincey shocked his
fellow countrymen with *Confessions of an English Opium
Eater*, a harrowing depiction of the addiction that blighted
his personal and professional life. The work remains a literary
classic. Both William Burroughs' *Junky* and Claude Brown's
Manchild in the Promised Land recount the travail of heroin
addicts during the 1950s.

Left: A portrait of the English Romantic poet John Keats, who took opium for medical and aesthetic purposes. Right: A drawing of Thomas DeQuincey, who chronicled the horrors of addiction in Confessions of an English Opium Eater.

The glories of wine are extolled in Omar Khayyám's *Rubaiyat*, a long poem written in 11th-century Persia. His most famous lines sing of "a loaf of bread, a jug of wine and thou." Five centuries later, William Shakespeare characterized a villain as "falser than vows made in wine." In Charles Dickens's *David Copperfield*, the character Mr. Micawber had trouble turning down a drink. But the hell of alcoholism was made more clear in two books of the 1940s — American novelist Charles R. Jackson's *Lost Weekend* and English novelist Malcolm Lowry's *Under the Volcano*.

Addiction As Side Effect

During the 19th century, many people, among them writers and artists, were introduced to opiates by their physician. In England during the Romantic era (late 18th–early 19th centuries) some of the country's greatest literary talents, including the poets Keats, Shelley, Byron, Coleridge, and the novelists Sir Walter Scott and Thomas De Quincey, took opiates for both medical and aesthetic purposes.

Sir Walter Scott was one notable who took laudanum for medicinal purposes yet managed to escape the snares of addiction. The drug was prescribed to him for abdominal complaints, but he regarded its effects as a nuisance that interfered with his work and social life. As soon as he was well, he renounced the mind-altering substance.

Samuel Taylor Coleridge, who took opium for rheumatic fever as well as anxiety and various aches and pains, had a love-hate relationship with the drug. The dreamlike quality and exotic imagery of some of his most famous poems, such as "Kubla Khan," *The Rime of the Ancient Mariner*, and "The Pains of Sleep," were no doubt influenced by the vivid dreams and heightened sensory perceptions of the opium experience. However, Coleridge was convinced that his opium habit had ruined his genius. He found, as most opium addicts do,

A bust of Sappho, the Greek lyric poet. Some scholars believe that she alluded to the effects of psychoactive substances in her writings.

that the heightened sensitivity faded away with continual use, leaving him with only his addiction. Although Coleridge was occasionally able to free himself of his dependency for periods of two or three months, for most of his life he drank two pints of laudanum a day.

Coleridge's friend Thomas De Quincey first took laudanum for a gastric ulcer and became fascinated by the way opium heightened his sensory perceptions and altered his sense of time. After his ulcer healed and he no longer needed opium for medication, he continued to set aside one evening a month when he took opium for the aesthetic pleasure it gave him. Unfortunately, after another ulcer attack in 1813, he once again had to use opium daily, struggling to keep his consumption down to one pint a day. As a result, he became addicted to the drug. After he married, he was able to taper off to a "thimblefull," but he never rid himself of the habit entirely.

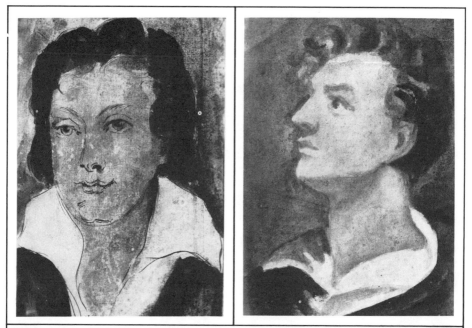

Watercolors by William Blake of the poets Shelley (left) and Byron. These Romantic poets sometimes fueled their search for fresh perspectives and novel experiences with opiates such as laudanum.

Elizabeth Barrett Browning (left) and Louisa May Alcott both took opium to treat physical maladies. Neither became addicted, but both incorporated their drug experiences in some of their writings.

As the 19th century wore on, doctors continued to prescribe opiates more or less indiscriminately. The poet Elizabeth Barrett Browning (1806–1861) began taking opium at the age of 15 after it was prescribed to treat a spinal injury. During that same time, Elizabeth Siddall, the wife of the English poet and painter Dante Gabriel Rossetti, became addicted to laudanum. One of the most famous artist's models in history, and herself an accomplished artist and poet, Siddall died from a laudanum overdose at the age of 28. Her husband died 10 years later from an overdose of chloral hydrate. The American writer Louisa May Alcott (1832–1888), best known for her novel *Little Women*, used opium and morphine to cope with the side effects of calomel, a very toxic mercury compound that was once prescribed to treat her typhoid pneumonia. Later, under different pen names, she wrote thrillers exploring the themes of drugs and violence.

The Modern Era

The 20th century is littered with creative figures who have succumbed to the temptations of drugs and alcohol as a means of managing physical and emotional stress. The great

Elizabeth Taylor battled addiction to alcohol and painkillers for years. Now recovered, she speaks openly of her illness and urges fellow victims to seek help as she did.

French cabaret singer Edith Piaf (1915–1963) was addicted to morphine; her American contemporary, jazz singer Billie Holiday (1915–1959) was addicted to heroin. More recently, such well-known entertainers as actress Elizabeth Taylor and singer Grace Slick, both dependent at one time on drugs and alcohol, have taken advantage of their high visibility to announce their recovery from addiction. Others have not been lucky enough to recover; their addictions have destroyed them. The gifted comic John Belushi's death from an overdose of heroin and cocaine in 1982 is a recent, tragic example.

Drugs and Waking Dreams

Of course, creative people take drugs for many of the same reasons that anyone else does. However, drugs may have some particular attractions for artists, writers, and entertainers. Probably the most common motivation is curiosity, a desire to expand the range of experience, consciousness, and knowledge. The altered states of consciousness induced by psychoactive drugs can be quite alluring to those who already see the world in vibrantly original ways.

Under the influence of some drugs, such as opium or the hallucinogens — LSD, psilocybin, or mescaline — many people claim to see visions or waking dreams. Their sense of time is altered, as it often is in dreams. Their sensory impressions may be very intense, drawing attention to a particular sound, object, or feeling with a heightened awareness.

Such experiences may be particularly significant to creative people seeking new insights and images to bring to their work. This was doubtless a factor that reinforced the drug dependencies of writers such as De Quincey, Coleridge, and Elizabeth Barrett Browning, who incorporated their drug experiences into their writings.

Jazz singer Billie Holiday, seen here leaving jail in 1956, was arrested several times on narcotics charges.

Most drugs also release people from their inhibitions to some extent. The behavior of many people is more spontaneous under the influence of a drug, and their thought patterns may also be less inhibited. The French poet Charles Baudelaire (1821–1867) experimented with the mind-expanding potential of drugs. Influenced by De Quincey's writings, he and his circle of artist and writer friends formed what they called "Le Club des Hashashins" (hashish eaters). They held gatherings where they tried the effects of opium and hashish on automatic writing, a process of writing very quickly without planning what one is to say. Baudelaire felt it was a way of recording as fully as possible the immediate effects of drugs.

Exploring New Worlds

When psychedelic or hallucinogenic drugs such as LSD and mescaline appeared in the 20th century, many writers turned to them in hopes that the radical perceptual changes these drugs induce might enhance creative vision. Under the guidance of a physician, British novelist and essayist Aldous Hux-

Aldous Huxley chronicled his experiences with mescaline in his 1954 book Doors of Perception.

ley took mescaline. French short story, journal, and novel writer Anaïs Nin took LSD.

These artists claimed to see rich and extraordinary visions under the influence of drugs. Huxley writes that while staring at an arrangement of flowers he experienced the "is-ness" of things. At one point, Anaïs Nin told the physician who was guiding her experience: "Without being a mathematician, I understood the infinite." Later, she wrote in her journal: "I found the origin of most of the images either in my work or in literary works by other writers ... in past dreams, in reading, in memories of travel, in actual experiences .... Therefore, I felt, the chemical did not reveal an unknown world. What it did was shut out the quotidian [ordinary] world as an interference and leave you alone with your dreams." Anaïs Nin concluded that her work in psychoanalysis, her own imaginative gifts, and her artistic discipline were the true source of her creativity, "not as a passing, ephemeral, vanishing dream, but as reality. And that is the conflict. The drug does not strengthen the desire to turn the dream, the vision, into reality. It is passive."

Many who have written about psychedelics point out that the quality of the experience depends on the expectations and capacities of the person who is taking the drug. In other words, even more so than with other drugs, the set and setting determine the experience. No drug can create artistry or genius in a person who does not already have these qualities. At most they can focus or rearrange creative patterns that are already present. The danger is that some people can use the passive drug experience as a substitute for the demanding work of creation.

The Pitfalls of Creativity

Lucy Barry Robe, in her book *Co-Starring Famous Women and Alcohol*, notes that the alcoholic and the writer have certain essential traits in common. Elaborating on this observation, one could draw some parallels between many artistic people and heavy drug users in general. One similarity derives from the compulsive nature of both drug taking and art making. For many who achieve success in their art, there is a need, a compulsion, to create. This need can be so overwhelming that it takes precedence over all other needs and activities. In a sense, artists are addicted to their work in the same way drug users are to their habit.

This may explain why many artists become addicted to drugs. The act of creation is a mind-changing experience, and the artist already has the ability and the need to be immersed in mind-changing experiences. Drug taking, in a sense, is what the poet William Butler Yeats once described as "creativity without toil."

Life Without Time Clocks

In addition to qualities of mind and personality that may make artists vulnerable to the lure of drugs, there is the practical side of the way they tend to structure their lives. An artist with a flexible schedule that does not include time clocks or nine-to-five workdays has time to indulge in drugs and re-cover from their effects. Actors, musicians, and other creative people who tend to work sporadically may fill in the nerve-racking time between projects by taking drugs. Also, show business and the creative arts tend to foster a group life-style that includes the use of alcohol and other drugs. This is par-ticularly true of musical groups whose members work to-gether, spend time on the road traveling together, and unwind together after a performance.

Many of these groups perform in bars, where the con-stant presence of alcohol is also a continual temptation to drink. Life on the road is exhausting, and stimulants keep the energy level up. In fact, during the 1920s and 1930s, long before cocaine and marijuana entered the mainstream of American life, these drugs were very popular with musicians, particularly black jazz musicians.

Like their counterparts in the music world, movie stars have long been notorious for their heavy use of alcohol and other drugs. All-night drinking bouts were a routine part of early film history, though this particular entertainment was somewhat dampened by the advent of the talkies. Instead of sipping and chatting until dawn, actors had to rush home after a day's shooting to learn the next day's lines. But, need-less to say, alcohol did not go out with the silent movie. Mind- and mood- altering substances continue to be part of

The Dutch artist Vincent van Gogh's Self Portrait with Flowered Wallpaper. *One of the most important of the post-impressionist painters, van Gogh was an alcoholic who eventually committed suicide.*

the Hollywood life-style. Like that of any other creative endeavor, the intense pressure of moviemaking pushes people to seek various means — including chemicals — to ease their tensions and boost their confidence.

One frequently finds an acute sensitivity in creative people. This sensitivity, when it results in heightened perception, is an asset to their work. In their personal lives, it can bring them great joy; however, sometimes it brings such intense pain they will go to great lengths to escape from it. For some artists, such as the 19th-century Dutch painter Vincent van Gogh (1853–90), this self-annihilation took the form of heavy drinking and eventually suicide.

Drug use as a means of coping with stress and insecurity is particularly dangerous because the people involved are often drinking, taking pills, or smoking to mask underlying problems. Because they do not confront and resolve their problems, the problems usually grow worse, and the unfortunate victim ends up with another problem — an addiction —to add to the original ones.

The American writer Susan Sontag has said that "it's probably a defense against anxiety that so many writers have been involved with drugs."

Writer's Block

Alcohol is also a traditional remedy for the occupational hazard known as "writer's block," a rather mysterious but very real affliction that makes it impossible for a writer to get anything down on paper. The block can last for years or for only a few hours or days when a writer is working on a project and gets stalled. At best, a drink or two can ease the writer's anxiety about the block; at worst, it can dam up the creative flow entirely. But it is a pretty sure thing that what gets dissolved by alcohol is the writer's discipline, not the writer's block.

The contemporary American woman of letters Susan Sontag, in an interview with *High Times* magazine, claims that she sometimes resorts to "a very mild form of speed" when she gets "really stuck" in her writing. When asked by the interviewer why she thought there was "this long history of writers and stimulants," Sontag replied, "I think there is something unnatural about writing in a room by yourself, and that it's quite natural that writers and also painters need something to get through all those hours and hours of being by yourself .... I think it's probably a defense against anxiety that so many writers have been involved in drugs."

Solitary work, of whatever nature, has its difficulties even for people who enjoy being by themselves. Drugs may seem to offer a substitute for companionship, cheering and stimulating the artist as a friend might. But in the end the "friend" usually proves to be false and unreliable; needed, perhaps, but not much help when it comes to getting on with life.

An 1882 book illustration shows the manufacture of opium in India. British trading companies made a fortune importing Indian opium into China but unleashed a plague of addiction on the Chinese people.

CHAPTER 4

DRUGS, TRADE, AND ECONOMICS

It has been estimated that the illegal drug trade represents an $80-billion-a-year industry in the 1980s; if the drug trade were a single company, it would rank second in sales to the Exxon Corporation, the nation's largest.

Erich Goodes, Drugs in American Society

At some point in history psychoactive substances have been commercially important to nearly every country. In fact, in many Third World nations today, the manufacture and trade of drugs are the largest industries. From the Opium Wars of the 1800s to the cocaine wars of the 1980s, drug wars are essentially trade wars, reflecting the status of drugs as enormously valuable commodities.

In light of the addictive properties of these drugs and their varied illegality over time, one might wonder why so many nations came to depend on their trade and why, in some countries, the plant forms of drugs are still the largest cash crops. The answers, perhaps, lie in the fact that the manufacture and sale of psychoactive substances have always been, and continue to be, highly profitable. This, coupled with an increasing demand for these substances, makes the profitability of the drug trade a matter of simple economics.

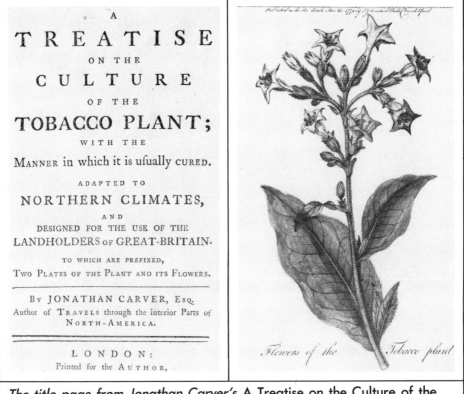

The title page from Jonathan Carver's A Treatise on the Culture of the Tobacco Plant, published in 1779. Indigenous to North America, tobacco was being cultivated the world over by the 17th century.

Tobacco and Alcohol: The Hidden Drugs

When Columbus landed in America, he found that the Indians put little rolls of dried leaves in their mouths and set them afire. Some also burned these leaves in pipes. It was evident to the early explorers that this smoking was essential to many religious and social rituals and was not easily given up.

In the 16th century, tobacco was brought to England, where it grew in popularity. By the beginning of the 17th century, tobacco plantations were springing up around the world. In America, the colony of Virginia flourished when it began a lucrative tobacco trade with England.

What the Indians had long known soon became apparent to early tobacco users: Once you started, you couldn't stop without severe discomfort and a powerful urge to resume the habit.

After King James I of England attempted to restrict the use of tobacco for health reasons, its value on the black market rose. This became a pattern that repeated itself throughout the world in other countries.

Obviously, attempts to stamp out tobacco use were not successful. The active and addictive ingredient nicotine in tobacco is today one of the most profitable of all legal drugs, earning about $16 billion per year in sales to U.S. smokers alone.

Like tobacco, alcohol has only recently been acknowledged as an addictive mind-altering drug. Although alcohol has been used as a part of both social and religious traditions for centuries, it was not often recognized as a substance both harmful and addictive. Though we now know this to be the case, most social drinkers would be astounded to hear their habit described as a form of casual drug use.

It is believed that the use of alcoholic beverages began as long ago as 6000 B.C.E. The ancient Romans were introduced to wine and viticulture, the cultivation of grapes, by

A detail from the 17th-century French artist Le Nain's The Smokers. *Although smoking was at one time quite respectable, the habit has lost popularity as evidence of nicotine's dangers has mounted.*

early Greek settlers. Soon after the Roman conquest of Italy, however, they turned to wine and wine making with a vengeance. By the 1st century B.C.E., wine had become Rome's most popular beverage, as well as a major export item and an important source of government revenue.

At the height of the Roman Empire, the economic fortune of Italy came to depend to a great extent on its vineyards. Not only had wine become the most important domestic industry, but concerted efforts were made to expand its sale beyond the peninsula.

After the fall of the Roman Empire, monks throughout Europe carried on and perfected the art of wine making. During the 12th and 13th centuries, the development of trade routes to and from the southern wine-producing countries helped to increase the consumption of wine in England and the Low Countries.

Alcoholic beverages have their place in American history as well. The trade of rum and whiskey helped to make the

An illustration from a medieval treatise on wine making, a process that was perfected by monks in Europe during the Middle Ages.

A 1929 lithograph depicts a speakeasy. Alcohol was available throughout Prohibition to those willing to pay outrageous prices.

coastal settlements of the New England colonies major trading ports. It also gave the colonists something to produce from all the surplus sugar they traded for with the West Indies, and the surplus corn they harvested from their own farms.

During Prohibition (1920–1933), popularity and prices of alcoholic beverages, despite the ban on drinking, were at an all-time high in America. Illegal smuggling, conducted by a growing network of organized crime figures, became big business. Private drinking clubs and "speakeasies" became the "in" places for those who could afford the exorbitant prices charged for good liquor. In the 1980s, alcoholic beverages are the basis of a multibillion dollar-a-year industry.

Opium: A Profitable Addiction

Opium first entered the world trade market around 333 B.C.E., when Alexander the Great carried it from Greece to Persia and India on his quest to extend his empire. Around 300 B.C.E., Arabian merchants carried opium poppies to East Asia.

During the 1500s, European merchants, enthusiastic over their introduction to tea in Asia, repaid the favor by introducing opium smoking to the Chinese. Up until that point, opium had been grown in China only in small quantities for medicinal purposes. By the onset of the 18th century, such companies as the Jardine Mathiesson Company of London and the British East India Company (chartered by the crown for trade with Asia), began to amass large fortunes from the brisk opium trade they conducted between India and China. The opium was grown in India, where it had been cultivated and used for centuries in folk medicine with few cases of addiction. The British traded Chinese tea for the Indian opium, which they then took back to China for sale at a huge profit.

The Opium Wars

The guardians of China's culture saw that opium wasted the lives of its smokers. It cost their nation silver and other trade commodities that it could ill afford, and it humbled the ancient Central Kingdom (as China was then called) before the mercenary West. (The West included the Americans who, to

A Greek coin stamped with the head of Alexander the Great. This Greek conqueror introduced opium into the world trade market around 333 B.C.E.

A Chinese scroll shows an official supervising the burning of opium. The Chinese waged two wars during the 19th century to halt the importation of opium into their country by British trading companies.

the great displeasure of the British, smuggled Turkish opium into China.) The smoke from opium dens, where users gathered to enjoy their pipes in secret, drifted over the coastlines and even rose above inland cities. Even the emperor's court had its smokers, as did all levels within the government and the army. By 1820 more than 300 tons of pure opium were imported annually. Ten years later, even after officials attempted harsh restrictions, the figure approached 2,000 tons a year. It is estimated that millions of Chinese were addicted to opium.

The British government was still convinced that more profit was possible from the opium traders. It revoked the charter of the British East India Company and acted directly to open Chinese ports to even more opium trade. The Chinese emperor was under strong pressure from his advisers to legalize opium. Although opium was still considered unsafe, the authorities hoped that through legislation, corruption and foreign influence could be minimized. But the emperor refused to legalize the drug. Instead, he began military preparations and ordered the executions of users and traffickers, foreign and domestic.

Workers harvest poppies in Southeast Asia. Local warlords control most of the opium trade in this part of the world.

The most notable effect of this policy was to anger the British. Within a year, the Opium War of 1839 began. When the Chinese lost the war three years later, they were forced to sign the Treaty of Nanking, which required them to pay large reparations and to surrender totally to British commercial interests. As a result, by 1852 opium imports had doubled. In 1856, with China under the rule of a new emperor, a second opium war began. This, however, brought China only more death, more reparations to pay, and more humiliation. Opium became officially legalized, and the Chinese ports were opened as never before to Western influences of every sort.

The Opium Wars have generated much analysis and historical commentary. Today many historians believe that opportunistic commercial interests had merely taken advantage of opium as a commodity — an especially insidious one to be sure — seeking any way to attain financial success. The clash between the expanding industrial powers of the West and the protective, tradition-bound culture of China might well have erupted eventually over some other commodity.

Opium Today: Heroin and High Profits

Today, the largest supply of opium comes from the Golden Triangle (Burma, Laos, and Thailand), the Golden Crescent (Pakistan, Iran, and Afghanistan), and Mexico. Nearly all the opium that is shipped out of producer countries is controlled by local warlords, men who vie among themselves for dominance over this vastly lucrative trade. This opium is either sold in its raw state or sent to laboratories to be processed and refined into morphine, heroin, or both.

Heroin production is also a profitable business. Each acre of opium poppies yields, at best, 10 kg, or about 22 lbs., of opium. The buyer pays local growers perhaps a few hundred dollars per acre, then takes the opium to be refined into morphine and further processed into heroin. Ten kg of opium would be equal to about one kg of either heroin or morphine. Each kilogram of heroin is worth several thousand dollars on the drug market, so the margin of profit for the manufacturer is very large.

Cocaine: A New Epidemic

Francisco Pizarro led the Spanish conquest of the Incan Empire in the 16th century. There the Spanish noted their Indian slaves' practice of chewing the leaves of the coca bush to give them energy. Though the conquistadors originally forbade this practice, they eventually realized that chewing the leaves gave their slaves remarkable powers of endurance, enabling them to work in the gold and silver mines with very little nourishment. Subsequently, the Spanish encouraged this use of coca. They also decided that coca chewing had great economic potential and began taxing it.

Today, of course, we are most familiar with the refined form of coca — cocaine — a highly addictive psychoactive drug. Coca, most of which is grown in South America, in its refined state is second only to marijuana as the most popular illicit drug in the world. It has become a multibillion-dollar global industry whose profits go mostly to the few men and groups who control production.

Eighty percent of the world's coca supply is grown in Peru and Bolivia. Bolivia, the poorest country in South America, has a per capita annual income of $470. Farmers there say the soil is too poor for growing crops other than coca, and they cultivate it in order to feed their families. For these farmers, growing coca is a means of economic survival. Coca is a cash crop that affords them an income in a country where unemployment is high and poverty extreme. The big profits, however, are not for the farmer but for the handful of criminals who run the cocaine empire.

Typically, the farmer who produces the coca is paid about $45 for 175 pounds of the leaves. When the leaves are soaked in kerosene, the resulting paste is worth $200. Sulfuric acid and alkali are then added to make a base worth $750. Finally, hydrochloric acid is added to produce cocaine, which is valued at $1,750 a pound. Crack, the rocklike pellets that form when baking soda and water are added, is valued at $5,500 a pound.

Colombia is the center of the cocaine industry. There, cartels, or criminal groups that control drug manufacture and trafficking, have their operating headquarters. These cocaine merchants are thought to be the wealthiest criminals in the world today.

The U.S. Drug Enforcement Administration (DEA) estimates that as much as 75% of Colombia's export earnings may come from the sale of illicit drugs. Illicit drug profits, which amount to almost incomprehensible amounts of cash, are deposited in numbered bank accounts in places such as the Bahamas or Panama, where the secrecy of bank activities is protected by law.

After the money is deposited in the numbered bank account, a "dummy" corporation, one that exists only on paper, is set up. A local lawyer handling the company's affairs then "lends" the money back to the dealer. As a result of such drug-related transactions, Panama, a small strip of land connecting Colombia and Costa Rica, has become the world's fourth largest banking center, after New York, London, and Hong Kong. In 1983 the Cayman Islands in the Caribbean

Workers synthesizing cocaine at an illicit laboratory in Peru are handcuffed after a police raid in 1986.

had 13,600 corporations registered — nearly one for every resident on the island — and in Panama, 200,000 corporations are on record.

But perhaps even more astounding than the high profits generated by cocaine are the number of deaths related to its trafficking. Judges, policemen, dealers, government officials, and innocent bystanders have all fallen victim to the cross fire unloosed by the cocaine empire. These drug wars have been initiated by various cartels in an attempt to gain control over production or distribution in a particular area, where no interference is tolerated from outside sources. Those who have dared to oppose these cartels have paid for it with their lives.

From alcohol and cigarettes to heroin and cocaine, drugs are big business — more profitable today than at any other time in history. Like all markets, the one for drugs is controlled by supply and demand. As long as the demand for psychoactive substances remains high, the merchants who satisfy this destructive but widespread craving will continue to flourish.

A 19th-century engraving captures the dream state of a man under the influence of ether. Discovered in the 1500s, ether was used for recreational purposes before being put to medical use in the 1800s.

CHAPTER 5

DRUGS, RECREATION, AND REBELLION

Humankind has put psychoactive drugs to various uses, both good and bad, throughout history. To be sure, the merely recreational use of drugs — the use of mind- and mood-altering substances for reasons that are neither medicinal nor tied to religious rituals — is more rampant in our time than in any other. However, former ages have seen their share of drug use in the interest either of enhancing experience or mitigating emotional suffering. Although there has never been a chemical solution for existential woes, the quest continues, but the results are invariably negative.

The drugs that every culture in every age have used for conviviality's sake run the gamut from mild to strong: from herbs to heroin, and from beer to 150-proof rum. As the drugs vary, so, too, do the kinds of social interactions they stimulate. These range from the wary camaraderie of a diplomatic dinner to the emotional bonding some people feel when sharing an illicit drug — passing a marijuana cigarette around at a party, for example.

The Most Ancient Drug

In our time, as in past ages, alcohol is the most widely used social drug. Beer is probably the oldest form of alcohol. Seven thousand years ago in Mesopotamia (later known as Persia, now called Iran), the Sumerians — people of Sumer, which was a part of Mesopotamia — developed a highly sophisticated culture. Among Sumer's legacies to later civilizations is the world's first written recipe for beer. However, archaeological evidence suggests that the art of beer making began earlier with Stone Age peoples, who produced narrow-necked storage vessels designed so that when the liquid mixture inside them fermented and formed carbon dioxide and alcohol, it would stay carbonated. That mixture, many experts insist, could only be beer.

If not beer, then wine is the oldest drug of human creation; both beer and wine production go so far back in history that exact dating is impossible. The first book of the Bible, Genesis, says that a vineyard was the first thing Noah planted after the Flood. The Sumerians, and later the Persians, Greeks, and Romans, all prized grape wine as a celebratory alcoholic drink. The Greeks who founded Marseilles in the 6th century B.C.E. taught the French how to grow grapes for wine; wherever Roman armies passed they introduced wine making.

A courtesan serves sake to a group of noblemen and other guests in this 18th-century Japanese woodcut. Sake, a rice wine, was first produced by the Chinese and was later adopted by the Japanese.

At about the time the Sumerians were first producing beer, the Chinese learned to ferment rice to produce wine and also to distill the wine into a kind of liquor called sake; in India the liquor *arak* was made from rice and sugar. Although the Greeks of classic times did not distill wine, they experimented with distilling turpentine to yield a drink probably similar to modern retsina. Meanwhile, the Celts, in what is now Scotland and Ireland, produced a crude whiskey that they called *uisegebaugh* — water of life. As British author and wine authority Alec Waugh commented 20 years ago, water of life was "a curious appellation for a concoction that many have maintained imperils man's prospects not only in this world but the next."

Cheaper than Gin

As we have seen, the 19th century was a time of great progress in the development of anesthetics and other drugs. However, no sooner would a drug make its appearance on the medical scene than it would be appropriated for social or recreational purposes. In fact, for a short time after ether and chloroform were developed, they were popular in Europe and America because they were cheaper to buy than alcohol; moreover, their inebriating effects could be enjoyed without the hangover that usually follows alcohol intoxication.

Because chloroform is highly toxic and an overdose can be fatal, it was in fashion for only a short period of time after its discovery. Ether was used recreationally (as opposed to surgically) at least as early as 1790 and during the mid-1800s was very popular in England and Ireland among people who had taken a temperance pledge but wanted a substitute for the pleasure they thought they had sacrificed in giving up gin. Ether also was free of the heavy tax that the British government had placed on spirits.

Nitrous oxide was at first used *only* for recreational purpose. Sniffing the gas produces an excitement followed by loud laughter — an effect that inspired its popular name, "laughing gas." Laughing-gas parties were a favorite amusement of English chemist Sir Humphry Davy, who first synthesized it, and his circle of poet and painter friends. American medical students took it up in the 1800s, and its recreational use continues to some extent today.

An 1808 cartoon satirizes the effects of "laughing gas," or nitrous oxide. This inhalant was used for its entertainment value long before it was used as an anesthetic.

Laudanum

These curious and dangerous alcohol substitutes, however, were by no means as popular as the alcohol-opium mixture most in demand in the 19th century — laudanum. An ounce of laudanum could be purchased for only a few pennies, and working-class people drank it to get high on Saturday night. Middle-class women used laudanum because alcohol drinking was considered inappropriate for women. Because whiskey can be detected on the breath and the signs of intoxication are fairly obvious, laudanum offered these women a way of imbibing in secrecy. In 19th-century America, in fact, the majority of laudanum users were white, middle-aged, middle-class women. Social attitudes toward laudanum use were fairly tolerant. Addicts were not considered a menace; unlike alcoholics, they were more likely to faint or fall asleep than to indulge in disruptive or violent behavior.

The Opium Den

Opium smoking was another matter, and the opium dens, or smoking houses, that sprang up in some English and American cities were considered disreputable. At first opium smoking in the United States was indulged in only by the Chinese laborers who immigrated to America in large numbers during the 1850s to build the transcontinental railways.

However, opium dens eventually became fashionable among young white people as well. In 1875 the city of San Francisco passed an ordinance forbidding the smoking of opium in dens. Other cities soon passed similar laws, spurred

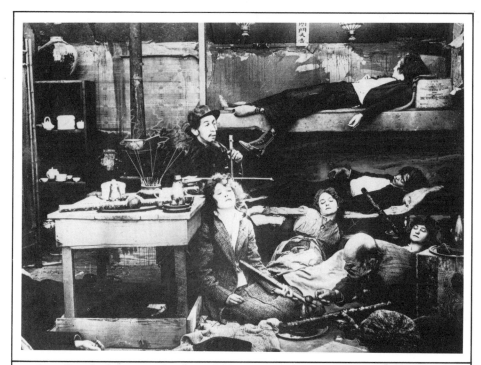

A stylized photograph of a 1920s opium den in New York City's Chinatown. Such haunts were commonplace during the late 19th and early 20th centuries, despite official efforts to shut them down.

by lurid stories in sensational newspapers that told of young girls who had been lured into prostitution while visiting opium dens. Despite the stories, the crackdown on these establishments seems to have been motivated more by hostility toward the Chinese, who were competing with whites for jobs, than by disapproval of the opium habit. Racially motivated or not, laws were enacted forbidding the use of opiates and cocaine.

Prohibition

In late 1919, the United States government passed a constitutional amendment prohibiting the sale of beverages containing more than 3.2% alcohol. Because whiskey was prohibited, ether again came to the fore as an alcohol substitute. More important, the fact that whiskey was forbidden made it especially attractive to many people. During the Roaring Twenties, gangsters took on the job of supplying the

Ben Shahn's 1934 gouache, Prohibition Alley. *Prohibition spawned an epidemic of violence, much of it masterminded by the gangster Al Capone, here depicted on a billboard overlooking kegs of whiskey.*

Rock star Jimi Hendrix was but one of many celebrities to fall victim to drug abuse. He died of a barbiturate overdose in 1970.

demand for "bootleg" booze (smuggled or illegally made whiskey). Gathering in speakeasies, as the illegal taverns were called, and drinking bootleg whiskey were the stylish things to do, especially for young people who found it a way to rebel against the authority of parents, teachers, and clergy. Previously law-abiding citizens began to make their own "bathtub gin." Prohibition proved so impossible to enforce that the amendment was repealed in 1933.

Marijuana

The practice of smoking marijuana was brought to Brazil by black slaves from Africa, spread to Mexico, and from there was brought to the United States by Mexican laborers. In the 1800s it was popular with black field hands in the South and in the hashish houses that often took the place of opium dens.

During the 1920s and 1930s, marijuana rose in popularity, especially among jazz musicians, most of whom were black. The term *reefer madness* was coined then to describe the effects of marijuana, which was believed to turn men into social deviants capable of crazed, even homicidal behavior. The violence of which they were supposed capable had more to do with white racist imaginings than with facts, for marijuana usually makes the user dreamy and self-absorbed. Nonetheless, marijuana was outlawed in 1937. Marijuana smoking became widespread in the 1960s. Legal or not, the slogan "tune in, turn on, drop out" was a rallying cry for many young people who were disillusioned with the social and ethical values of their elders. Smoking marijuana became a form of protest.

Should Recreational Drug Use Be Legalized?

Although "turning on" is out of style, drugs still represent rebellion. For many, curtailing their use conflicts with the democratic ideals of civil liberty. For this reason, some people advocate the legalization of all drugs. Others would legalize marijuana alone. Most believe the present laws should be kept in force and perhaps strengthened.

Those who advocate universal legalization argue that making drugs illegal enhances their allure and turns people who use them into criminals. When drugs are illegal, their prices are inflated; users often turn to crime — becoming thieves, embezzlers, and prostitutes—to buy drugs.

Illegal drugs are available only from representatives of organized crime, who reap huge sums of money from their sale. Legalizing and taxing drugs would provide revenue to the government as the taxes paid on cigarettes and alcohol do now. The purity of legal drugs could be controlled, thus helping to avoid some of the dangers of street drugs.

Those who oppose the legalization of drugs argue that if they were legal, they would as a consequence be widely available and relatively inexpensive. More people would be encouraged to use them. They point out that alcohol, which is legal, is the most widely used of any drug and is linked to more traffic accidents, fatalities, and violent crimes than any other drug.

Conclusion

The use — and overuse — of drugs has very complicated social and cultural roots. Some people avoid them altogether. A very few use drugs sparingly and intelligently. Others, however, repeatedly seek escape from their problems in drugs. Stress, insecurity, poverty, unemployment, loneliness, boredom — all these are factors that may lead people to experiment with drugs.

As every user learns, though, drugs are somewhat like the magic genies who lived in bottles in fairy tales. When they were released, they could use their enormous powers to do good or cause destruction. What happened after the bottle was uncorked had a great deal to do with the nature of the genie, but it had even more to do with its master; one might be foolish, and send the genie on useless or evil errands, another wise, and use the genie well. But the wisest master of all was the one who left the bottled-up genie alone.

APPENDIX

State Agencies
for the Prevention and Treatment
of Drug Abuse

ALABAMA

Department of Mental Health
Division of Mental Illness and
 Substance Abuse Community
 Programs
200 Interstate Park Drive
P.O. Box 3710
Montgomery, AL 36193
(205) 271-9253

ALASKA

Department of Health and Social
 Services
Office of Alcoholism and Drug
 Abuse
Pouch H-05-F
Juneau, AK 99811
(907) 586-6201

ARIZONA

Department of Health Services
Division of Behavioral Health
 Services
Bureau of Community Services
Alcohol Abuse and Alcoholism
 Section
2500 East Van Buren
Phoenix, AZ 85008
(602) 255-1238

Department of Health Services
Division of Behavioral Health
 Services
Bureau of Community Services
Drug Abuse Section
2500 East Van Buren
Phoenix, AZ 85008
(602) 255-1240

ARKANSAS

Department of Human Services
Office of Alcohol and Drug Abuse
 Prevention
1515 West 7th Avenue
Suite 310
Little Rock, AR 72202
(501) 371-2603

CALIFORNIA

Department of Alcohol and Drug
 Abuse
111 Capitol Mall
Sacramento, CA 95814
(916) 445-1940

COLORADO

Department of Health
Alcohol and Drug Abuse Division
4210 East 11th Avenue
Denver, CO 80220
(303) 320-6137

CONNECTICUT

Alcohol and Drug Abuse
 Commission
999 Asylum Avenue
3rd Floor
Hartford, CT 06105
(203) 566-4145

DELAWARE

Division of Mental Health
Bureau of Alcoholism and Drug
 Abuse
1901 North Dupont Highway
Newcastle, DE 19720
(302) 421-6101

DISTRICT OF COLUMBIA
Department of Human Services
Office of Health Planning and
  Development
601 Indiana Avenue, NW
Suite 500
Washington, D.C. 20004
(202) 724-5641

FLORIDA
Department of Health and
  Rehabilitative Services
Alcoholic Rehabilitation Program
1317 Winewood Boulevard
Room 187A
Tallahassee, FL 32301
(904) 488-0396

Department of Health and
  Rehabilitative Services
Drug Abuse Program
1317 Winewood Boulevard
Building 6, Room 155
Tallahassee, FL 32301
(904) 488-0900

GEORGIA
Department of Human Resources
Division of Mental Health and
  Mental Retardation
Alcohol and Drug Section
618 Ponce De Leon Avenue, NE
Atlanta, GA 30365-2101
(404) 894-4785

HAWAII
Department of Health
Mental Health Division
Alcohol and Drug Abuse Branch
1250 Punch Bowl Street
P.O. Box 3378
Honolulu, HI 96801
(808) 548-4280

IDAHO
Department of Health and Welfare
Bureau of Preventive Medicine
Substance Abuse Section
450 West State
Boise, ID 83720
(208) 334-4368

ILLINOIS
Department of Mental Health and
  Developmental Disabilities
Division of Alcoholism
160 North La Salle Street
Room 1500
Chicago, IL 60601
(312) 793-2907

Illinois Dangerous Drugs
  Commission
300 North State Street
Suite 1500
Chicago, IL 60610
(312) 822-9860

INDIANA
Department of Mental Health
Division of Addiction Services
429 North Pennsylvania Street
Indianapolis, IN 46204
(317) 232-7816

IOWA
Department of Substance Abuse
505 5th Avenue
Insurance Exchange Building
Suite 202
Des Moines, IA 50319
(515) 281-3641

KANSAS
Department of Social Rehabilitation
Alcohol and Drug Abuse Services
2700 West 6th Street
Biddle Building
Topeka, KS 66606
(913) 296-3925

KENTUCKY
Cabinet for Human Resources
Department of Health Services
Substance Abuse Branch
275 East Main Street
Frankfort, KY 40601
(502) 564-2880

LOUISIANA
Department of Health and Human
  Resources
Office of Mental Health and
  Substance Abuse
655 North 5th Street
P.O. Box 4049
Baton Rouge, LA 70821
(504) 342-2565

MAINE
Department of Human Services
Office of Alcoholism and Drug
  Abuse Prevention
Bureau of Rehabilitation
32 Winthrop Street
Augusta, ME 04330
(207) 289-2781

MARYLAND
Alcoholism Control Administration
201 West Preston Street
Fourth Floor
Baltimore, MD 21201
(301) 383-2977

State Health Department
Drug Abuse Administration
201 West Preston Street
Baltimore, MD 21201
(301) 383-3312

MASSACHUSETTS
Department of Public Health
Division of Alcoholism
755 Boylston Street
Sixth Floor
Boston, MA 02116
(617) 727-1960

Department of Public Health
Division of Drug Rehabilitation
600 Washington Street
Boston, MA 02114
(617) 727-8617

MICHIGAN
Department of Public Health
Office of Substance Abuse Services
3500 North Logan Street
P.O. Box 30035
Lansing, MI 48909
(517) 373-8603

MINNESOTA
Department of Public Welfare
Chemical Dependency Program
  Division
Centennial Building
658 Cedar Street
4th Floor
Saint Paul, MN 55155
(612) 296-4614

MISSISSIPPI
Department of Mental Health
Division of Alcohol and Drug Abuse
1102 Robert E. Lee Building
Jackson, MS 39201
(601) 359-1297

MISSOURI
Department of Mental Health
Division of Alcoholism and Drug
  Abuse
2002 Missouri Boulevard
P.O. Box 687
Jefferson City, MO 65102
(314) 751-4942

MONTANA
Department of Institutions
Alcohol and Drug Abuse Division
1539 11th Avenue
Helena, MT 59620
(406) 449-2827

NEBRASKA
Department of Public Institutions
Division of Alcoholism and Drug
Abuse
801 West Van Dorn Street
P.O. Box 94728
Lincoln, NB 68509
(402) 471-2851, Ext. 415

NEVADA
Department of Human Resources
Bureau of Alcohol and Drug Abuse
505 East King Street
Carson City, NV 89710
(702) 885-4790

NEW HAMPSHIRE
Department of Health and Welfare
Office of Alcohol and Drug Abuse
    Prevention
Hazen Drive
Health and Welfare Building
Concord, NH 03301
(603) 271-4627

NEW JERSEY
Department of Health
Division of Alcoholism
129 East Hanover Street CN 362
Trenton, NJ 08625
(609) 292-8949

Department of Health
Division of Narcotic and Drug
    Abuse Control
129 East Hanover Street CN 362
Trenton, NJ 08625
(609) 292-8949

NEW MEXICO
Health and Environment Department
Behavioral Services Division
Substance Abuse Bureau
725 Saint Michaels Drive
P.O. Box 968
Santa Fe, NM 87503
(505) 984-0020, Ext. 304

NEW YORK
Division of Alcoholism and Alcohol
    Abuse
194 Washington Avenue
Albany, NY 12210
(518) 474-5417

Division of Substance Abuse
    Services
Executive Park South
Box 8200
Albany, NY 12203
(518) 457-7629

NORTH CAROLINA
Department of Human Resources
Division of Mental Health, Mental
    Retardation and Substance Abuse
    Services
Alcohol and Drug Abuse Services
325 North Salisbury Street
Albemarle Building
Raleigh, NC 27611
(919) 733-4670

NORTH DAKOTA
Department of Human Services
Division of Alcoholism and Drug
    Abuse
State Capitol Building
Bismarck, ND 58505
(701) 224-2767

OHIO
Department of Health
Division of Alcoholism
246 North High Street
P.O. Box 118
Columbus, OH 43216
(614) 466-3543

Department of Mental Health
Bureau of Drug Abuse
65 South Front Street
Columbus, OH 43215
(614) 466-9023

OKLAHOMA
Department of Mental Health
Alcohol and Drug Programs
4545 North Lincoln Boulevard
Suite 100 East Terrace
P.O. Box 53277
Oklahoma City, OK 73152
(405) 521-0044

OREGON
Department of Human Resources
Mental Health Division
Office of Programs for Alcohol and
Drug Problems
2575 Bittern Street, NE
Salem, OR 97310
(503) 378-2163

PENNSYLVANIA
Department of Health
Office of Drug and Alcohol
Programs
Commonwealth and Forster Avenues
Health and Welfare Building
P.O. Box 90
Harrisburg, PA 17108
(717) 787-9857

RHODE ISLAND
Department of Mental Health,
Mental Retardation and Hospitals
Division of Substance Abuse
Substance Abuse Administration
Building
Cranston, RI 02920
(401) 464-2091

SOUTH CAROLINA
Commission on Alcohol and Drug
Abuse
3700 Forest Drive
Columbia, SC 29204
(803) 758-2521

SOUTH DAKOTA
Department of Health
Division of Alcohol and Drug Abuse
523 East Capitol, Joe Foss Building
Pierre, SD 57501
(605) 773-4806

TENNESSEE
Department of Mental Health and
Mental Retardation
Alcohol and Drug Abuse Services
505 Deaderick Street
James K. Polk Building,
Fourth Floor
Nashville, TN 37219
(615) 741-1921

TEXAS
Commission on Alcoholism
809 Sam Houston State Office
Building
Austin, TX 78701
(512) 475-2577
Department of Community Affairs
Drug Abuse Prevention Division
2015 South Interstate Highway 35
P.O. Box 13166
Austin, TX 78711
(512) 443-4100

UTAH
Department of Social Services
Division of Alcoholism and Drugs
150 West North Temple
Suite 350
P.O. Box 2500
Salt Lake City, UT 84110
(801) 533-6532

VERMONT
Agency of Human Services
Department of Social and
Rehabilitation Services
Alcohol and Drug Abuse Division
103 South Main Street
Waterbury, VT 05676
(802) 241-2170

VIRGINIA
Department of Mental Health and
  Mental Retardation
Division of Substance Abuse
109 Governor Street
P.O. Box 1797
Richmond, VA 23214
(804) 786-5313

WASHINGTON
Department of Social and Health
  Service
Bureau of Alcohol and Substance
  Abuse
Office Building—44 W
Olympia, WA 98504
(206) 753-5866

WEST VIRGINIA
Department of Health
Office of Behavioral Health Services
Division on Alcoholism and Drug
  Abuse
1800 Washington Street East
Building 3 Room 451
Charleston, WV 25305
(304) 348-2276

WISCONSIN
Department of Health and Social
  Services
Division of Community Services
Bureau of Community Programs
Alcohol and Other Drug Abuse
  Program Office
1 West Wilson Street
P.O. Box 7851
Madison, WI 53707
(608) 266-2717

WYOMING
Alcohol and Drug Abuse Programs
Hathaway Building
Cheyenne, WY 82002
(307) 777-7115, Ext. 7118

GUAM
Mental Health & Substance Abuse
  Agency
P.O. Box 20999
Guam 96921

PUERTO RICO
Department of Addiction Control
  Services
Alcohol Abuse Programs
P.O. Box B-Y Rio Piedras Station
Rio Piedras, PR 00928
(809) 763-5014

Department of Addiction Control
  Services
Drug Abuse Programs
P.O. Box B-Y Rio Piedras Station
Rio Piedras, PR 00928
(809) 764-8140

VIRGIN ISLANDS
Division of Mental Health,
  Alcoholism & Drug Dependency
  Services
P.O. Box 7329
Saint Thomas, Virgin Islands 00801
(809) 774-7265

AMERICAN SAMOA
LBJ Tropical Medical Center
Department of Mental Health Clinic
Pago Pago, American Samoa 96799

TRUST TERRITORIES
Director of Health Services
Office of the High Commissioner
Saipan, Trust Territories 96950

Further Reading

Benedict, Ruth. *Patterns of Culture*. New York: New American Library, 1934.

Califano, Joseph A., Jr. *Drug Abuse and Alcoholism*. New York: Warner Books, 1982.

Frazer, Sir James. *The Golden Bough*. New York: Macmillan, 1920.

Gill, Sam M. *Native American Religions*. California: Wadsworth, 1982.

Goode, Erich. *Drugs in American Society*. New York: Knopf, 1984.

Grinspoon, Lester, and James B. Bakalar. *Cocaine: A Drug and Its Social Evolution*. New York: Basic Books, 1985.

Huxley, Aldous. *Collected Essays*. New York: Bantam Books, 1960.

Lattimer, Dean, and Jeff Goldberg. *Flowers in the Blood: The Story of Opium*. New York: Franklin Watts, 1981.

Nellis, Muriel. *The Female Fix*. New York: Penguin Books, 1980.

Palmer, Cynthia, and Michael Horowitz. *Shaman Woman, Mainline Lady*. New York: Morrow, 1972.

Robe, Lucy Barry. *Co-Starring Famous Women and Alcohol*. Minneapolis, MN: CompCare Publications, 1986.

Sloman, Larry. *Reefer Madness: The History of Marijuana in America*. New York: Bobbs-Merrill, 1979.

Trebach, Arnold S. *The Heroin Solution*. New Haven, CT: Yale University Press, 1982.

Wasson, Robert Gordon, Albert Hoffman, and Carl A. P. Ruch. *The Road to Eleusis*. Harcourt Brace Jovanovitch, 1978.

Weil, Andrew, M.D. *Chocolate to Morphine*. Boston: Houghton Mifflin, 1983.

Glossary

addiction a condition caused by repeated drug use, characterized by a compulsive urge to continue using the drug, a tendency to increase the dosage, and physiological and/or psychological dependence

adulterate to add an extra ingredient to a pure substance, increasing the bulk but decreasing the quality of the substance

alcoholism chronic alcohol abuse often resulting in serious deterioration of mental and physical health

amphetamine a drug that stimulates the central nervous system, alleviates fatigue, and produces a feeling of alertness and well-being. Although it has been used for weight control, repeated use of the drug can cause restlessness and insomnia

analgesic a drug that reduces or eliminates pain

barbiturate a drug that causes depression of the central nervous system; generally used to reduce anxiety or induce euphoria

carcinogen a cancer-causing substance

chemotherapy a form of cancer treatment in which the patient is given toxic chemicals to kill the cancer cells

cocaine the primary psychoactive ingredient in the coca plant; it functions as a behavioral stimulant

coma deep unconsciousness that may last for hours, days, or even years

convulsion a violent contraction of the muscles

delirium tremens a condition caused by abrupt withdrawal of a drug, usually alcohol, characterized by violent trembling and hallucinations; also called "DTs"

depressant a drug that reduces the activity of the central nervous system

depression a mental condition characterized by sadness, dejection, and apathy

distillation a process where liquid is repeatedly heated to purify or separate a complex mixture, causing the remaining liquid to become more concentrated

endorphins compounds produced in the brain that serve as the body's natural opiates

euphoria a mental high characterized by a feeling of well-being

hallucination sensory perceptions that have no basis in reality

hallucinogen a drug that causes the user to experience hallucinations

Harrison Narcotics Act a law passed in 1914 requiring that all sales of opiates and cocaine be registered.

heroin a semisynthetic opiate produced by a chemical modification of morphine

lysergic acid diethylamide a hallucinogenic drug derived from a fungus that grows on rye or from morning-glory seeds

morphine an addictive drug derived from opium and used as a sedative or anesthetic

narcotic originally a group of drugs producing effects similar to those of morphine; often used to refer to any substance that sedates, has a depressive effect, and/or causes dependence

opiate any compound from the milky juice of the poppy plant *Papaver somniferum*, including opium, morphine, codeine, and heroin

physical dependence an adaption of the body to the presence of a drug such that its absence produces withdrawal symptoms

pituitary gland a small oval gland at the base of the brain; its secretions stimulate other glands

psychedelic producing hallucinations or having mind-altering properties

psychoanalysis a method of treating mental illness by recognizing and analyzing subconscious thoughts

psychological dependence a condition in which the drug user craves a drug to maintain a sense of well-being and feels discomfort when deprived of it

psychosis mental diseases characterized by hallucinations, mood disturbances, and a loss of contact with reality

resin a sticky substance found in plants

sensory deprivation tank a lightproof, soundproof tank filled with warm water that people use for relaxing and exploring altered states of mind

stimulant a substance that accelerates physiological or organic activity

synthesize to combine chemicals to create a new substance

tuberculosis a contagious respiratory disease

tolerance a decrease in susceptibility to the effects of a drug due to its continued administration, resulting in the user's need to increase the drug dosage in order to achieve the effects experienced previously

withdrawal the physiological and psychological effects of discontinued use of a drug

Index

Sally Freeman is a writer and former editor of *Natural Lifestyles* magazine. She is coauthor and editor of *The Green World* and *The Kitchen Almanac,* both published by Berkeley Books, and has also been contributing editor for Cambridge Books' *On The Job* series. She has written on various topics for *Parents, Prevention, Fitness for Living* and other national publications. Ms. Freeman lives in Brooklyn and is writing a novel for children based on mythological themes.

Solomon H. Snyder, M.D. is Distinguished Service Professor of Neuroscience, Pharmacology and Psychiatry at The Johns Hopkins University School of Medicine. He has served as president of the Society for Neuroscience and in 1978 received the Albert Lasker Award in Medical Research. He has authored *Uses of Marijuana, Madness and the Brain, The Troubled Mind, Biological Aspects of Mental Disorder,* and edited *Perspective in Neuropharmacology: A Tribute to Julius Axelrod.* Professor Snyder was a research associate with Dr. Axelrod at the National Institutes of Health.

Barry L. Jacobs, Ph.D., is currently a professor in the program of neuroscience at Princeton University. Professor Jacobs is author of *Serotonin Neurotransmission and Behavior* and *Hallucinogens: Neurochemical, Behavioral and Clinical Perspectives.* He has written many journal articles in the field of neuroscience and contributed numerous chapters to books on behavior and brain science. He has been a member of several panels of the National Institute of Mental Health.

Joann Ellison Rodgers, M.S. (Columbia), became Deputy Director of Public Affairs and Director of Media Relations for the Johns Hopkins Medical Institutions in Baltimore, Maryland, in 1984 after 18 years as an award-winning science journalist and widely read columnist for the Hearst newspapers.